HOW TO PASS

THE CIVIL SERVICE QUALIFYING TESTS

The essential guide for clerical
and Fast Stream applicants

3rd edition

MIKE BRYON

KOGAN
PAGE

Publisher's note
Every possible effort has been made to ensure that the information contained in this book is accurate at the time of going to press, and the publishers and author cannot accept responsibility for any errors or omissions, however caused. No responsibility for loss or damage occasioned to any person acting, or refraining from action, as a result of the material in this publication can be accepted by the editor, the publisher or the author.

First published in Great Britain in 1995 by Kogan Page Limited
Reprinted 1997, 1998, 1999
Second edition 2003
Reprinted 2003, 2005
Third edition 2007

120 Pentonville Road
London N1 9JN
United Kingdom
www.kogan-page.co.uk

© Mike Bryon, 1995, 2003, 2007

British Library Cataloguing in Publication Data

A CIP record for this book is available from the British Library.

ISBN-10   0 7494 4853 9
ISBN-13   978 0 7494 4853 0

Typeset by Saxon Graphics Ltd, Derby
Printed and bound in Great Britain by Creative Print and Design (Wales), Ebbw Vale

Contents

iv How to pass the Civil Service qualifying tests

Preface

Use this book to find your way successfully through the initial stages of the UK Civil Service ordinary entry or Fast Steam recruitment process. It has been developed expressly for the purpose of helping prepare for the Civil Service Qualifying Exams.

This edition has been completely updated. It contains harder practice questions. There is new material on online tests, on following procedure and speed and accuracy, as well as e-tray exercises, written exercises and assessment days. It offers well over 100 tips and insights into the Fast Stream competition and, in response to readers' requests, provides more and fuller explanations.

If you are about to take a Civil Service test, first establish that the practice questions contained here are indeed relevant to the test that you face. The department or agency to whom you have applied should have directed you to a description of its test and a number of sample questions. It is essential that you study this information carefully and, before you spend time on these exercises, establish that this material is relevant to the real questions. This book is a learning aid and contains material intended to help you reach the standard demanded by the real tests and master the competencies tested in them. To aid learning, sections usually start with questions easier than those found in the real test.

To do well in Civil Service tests, many people need to set about quite a major programme of revision. You may need more practice material than contained in this book. There are many other good sources, some online as well as other books.

If you are finding it difficult to identify sufficient relevant practice material, then by all means e-mail me care of Kogan Page, providing details of the Civil Service test that you face and an e-mail address on which you can be contacted. I will be glad to inform you of any other source that I know.

I apologize in advance if you discover any errors in these practice questions; try not to allow it to undermine your confidence in the value of practice and please do not take too dim a view of the rest of the book, because it definitely does contain lots of worthwhile practice material. I have tried hard to keep errors out and I hope I have not missed too many. I will be glad to hear of any, care of Kogan Page, in order that they can be removed at the next reprint.

Acknowledgements

The first edition of this book was written with the encouragement and support of staff from the Recruitment and Assessment Services, at that time a department of the Cabinet Office. Previous editions have helped tens of thousands of applicants to prepare for the Civil Service qualifying tests. The idea formed over 12 years ago and came from my work for departments of the Civil Service supporting many hundreds of candidates in their application to the service. If you find this book helpful, it is because of the insights provided to me by those individuals, many of whom are now working in the service. I am indebted to them. The Civil Service tests are in an almost constant state of development and I am also indebted to the many readers who have contacted me for advice when new styles of test and question appear.

The views expressed are not those of the government, any department of the Civil Service or any serving civil servant. The practice questions are not from past papers and are not real Civil Service exam questions; they and the advice offered have been written and used to help real candidates pass the real tests. Any errors or omissions are entirely mine.

May I take this opportunity to wish you every success in your attempt to join the Civil Service, and in particular in meeting the challenge of the qualifying tests.

The Civil Service, the tests and practice

Administrative staff in the Civil Service

Why is it that people routinely work to improve their CV or interview technique, but few seek to improve their performance in employers' tests?

This book is packed with insights and practice questions. Use it to fulfil your dream of winning a vital and influential position within the Civil Service.

Too few candidates realize that they can improve their scores in these common assessments. Occupational psychologists accept that a lack of familiarity with tests, low self-esteem, nervousness or a lack of confidence will result in a lower score. It is equally true to say that hard work, determination and, most of all, systematic preparation can lead to a significant improvement in performance. For some candidates, practice will mean the difference between passing and failing.

Civil servants are officials who work for a minister of the government of the day. They work in departments and agencies of central government, developing and implementing policies. Employees of the police, local government and the armed services are not civil servants.

Civil servants are politically impartial and the service is non-political. Governments change but the service remains unaffected and will serve whichever government is elected.

Administrators in the service are in an important respect considered to be generalists. After a qualifying period, and once you reach the higher grades, you may gain experience of all aspects of administration and move between specialist functions periodically. The experience gained from each function is considered to be transferable, and you will be expected to be able to learn quickly and to be flexible. Training is primarily on the job. In recent years the service has undergone considerable change; structures used to be centrally defined but this no longer necessarily applies throughout the service. Increasingly, civil servants are occupied with the development and implementation of the policies of the European Union as well as those of Parliament.

A major effort has been made to locate parts of departments and most of the executive agencies outside the capital. This has meant that fewer civil servants are located in London and the South East region generally.

Another change has been the provision of information about the service and vacancies on the internet. This is a vital source of information, especially in terms of the type of work available and the recruitment process, including any tests. The internet makes it far easier to keep the information up to date and provides a very cost-effective means of providing a great deal of information. There is little point in attempting to repeat or summarize this material here. See 'Further information' for useful Web addresses.

Up until now, the terms and conditions of employment of civil servants have been explained in a substantial, rigorous and clearly written publication called *The Civil Service Staff*

Handbook. Although in recent years, the prospects of promotion have reduced considerably, all staff benefit from annual appraisals which include an assessment of whether or not they are 'fit' for promotion.

It is a legal requirement that recruitment to the service is by fair and open competition and that selection and promotion are on the basis of merit alone. Fairness and openness mean that the service is required to ensure that vacancies are widely publicized, and this often results in very large numbers of applications. To ensure fairness each applicant must be given proper and due consideration, which takes a considerable amount of time and resources.

The process used to recruit to the service usually comprises most or all of the following features:

1. Applicants are referred to information about the vacancies and departments. The intention is to allow candidates to make an informed decision over whether or not to proceed with their application.
2. Self-assessments are used to further help applicants to decide if they are suited to the service.
3. Through an application form, sufficient information is obtained to sift the candidates on the basis of a set of criteria agreed in advance and considered essential to the post. It is common for many candidates to be rejected at this stage, so take care to present your experience as relevant and minimize the number of errors on your form.
4. One or a series of questionnaires may be used that ask questions about your working style and personality. These are used to determine whether candidates are suited to a career in the service.
5. Applicants may have to pass a set of standardized tests, which are administered either online or to large groups of applicants.
6. The next stage in the process may include an e-tray exercise. This is a type of work-sample test that resembles a 'Microsoft Outlook' inbox containing background files

that receives a series of 'e-mails' to which the candidate must respond.
7. Candidates who have successfully passed the sift stages may be required to attend an assessment centre where they undertake work-related exercises, discussion groups, written assignments, interviews and the preparation and delivery of a presentation.
8. Panel interviews are conducted.

The service is an acknowledged leader in the field of providing childcare support, career-break schemes and job-sharing arrangements. I have first-hand experience of working with civil servants who take equality of opportunity very seriously and work hard to ensure a fair and equitable system of recruitment and management.

There have been considerable and genuine efforts, coordinated by the Cabinet Office, to address issues of representation.

The Cabinet Office continually monitors the service's recruitment processes, including the qualifying exams, for bias, and takes measures to guard against any unintentional racial or gender discrimination. No system is perfect, but candidates should take some assurance from the fact that the service is ahead of the majority of British industries, operates a relatively equitable recruitment process, and in this respect represents a better employer than most.

A programme of validity studies is carried out to demonstrate that the selected candidates go on to be successful in the Civil Service.

The *Fast Stream Report 2005* found that candidates who described their ethnicity as black or as belonging to an ethnic minority group were disproportionately unsuccessful at the qualifying test stage and that people with a disability were successful in broadly the same proportions as they applied, but only a small number applied in the first instance.

Tests and practice

Let's deal with a few still common misconceptions: If you fail one of the Civil Service qualifying test it does not mean that you lack the potential to be a civil servant. They do not somehow test your innate ability and you can markedly improve your score through practice. Most successful candidates have practised before they take a Civil Service test. Many, many pass them only after two or more attempts. Most go on to prove themselves to be very able civil servants.

When tests are used to select and reject applicants, they leave you as a candidate with no alternative but to try to earn the very best possible score. When there are lots of candidates and relatively few vacancies, then like it or not you have entered a competition. In many instances a fierce competition. You must do better than most other candidates in order to be selected for the next stage in the recruitment process.

Two things will help you succeed. First, realize that practice prior to the test is essential if you are to become familiar with the test demands, build up speed and avoid common mistakes. Second, you must realize that doing well in a test is not simply down to intelligence; you must also be sufficiently motivated to want to pass and to try very hard, both before the test and during the test itself. In some cases, practice and a determination to do well will mean you succeed when you would otherwise have not.

All employers' tests, including those used by the Civil Service, owe much of their heritage to attempts early in the last century to measure intelligence. We are all familiar with the notion of IQ (intelligence quotient) and how a score is offered as a measurement of an individual's intelligence; a score of 100 is deemed average, while a score of over 160 might indicate genius. Pioneers of testing predicted that we would no longer have to wait for the lessons of experience to discover how well suited anybody was for a particular career or educational path. Instead we would be able to attribute scores to individuals and be able to tell who was best suited for a particular career or for a place in, for example, higher education.

It was soon realized that these early tests failed to predict success in particular careers or higher education. Intelligence is a complex and controversial notion that has proved very difficult to define. The concept of intelligence adopted by the early testers was crude, and related to only a few of the items that affect the complexities of understanding intelligence. The early tests were primarily concerned with the measurement of verbal ability and the handling of numerical, pictorial and geometric relations.

The validity of these early tests was much exaggerated, and this gave rise to considerable scepticism and some hostility towards testing. There had, of course, been more sober commentators, and the views of these individuals came to the fore. In particular, it was stressed that someone's score should be taken not as an indication of overall intelligence, but simply as a measurement of that individual's ability in the aptitude tested. Some IQ tests were renamed ability tests and redesigned to measure single aptitudes more specifically. Instead of attributing a single score, tests offered a profile of scores in various abilities. In other cases an individual's score was compared with the normal score of other candidates with similar backgrounds. These tests are in essence the precursors of the tests used today by employers. Considerable and lengthy studies are undertaken in order to quantify the predictive value of such tests.

Today these tests are written by occupational psychologists who go to considerable lengths to achieve objectivity by applying standard scientific methods and statistical techniques to the task of deciding between candidates. This is not to say that the tests are perfect; in fact the vast majority are not. However, the resulting psychometric scores are considered by many to be the best single predictor of likely job performance.

Notification that you were unsuccessful may mean nothing more than that you did not do well enough in the competition on that occasion. You should certainly not conclude that failure to pass a qualifying exam means that you are unsuitable for employment as a civil servant. In some instances so many people apply and there are so few vacancies that even very able candidates are rejected. So do not immediately rethink your career plans. Try again after doing more practice. If you repeatedly fail, try to establish if any alternative routes exist into the employment of your choice. It may be that holders of particular qualifications do not have to sit the exam, or you may be able to join the department at a more junior grade and seek promotion.

A winning approach

The best frame of mind in which to approach a qualifying exam is to treat it as an opportunity to demonstrate your true worth. Avoid any feelings of resentment over the fact that you have to take a test. Do not fear failure but instead concentrate on the opportunity to pass. Have confidence in yourself. Realize that you have nothing to lose if you try your best and really go for it.

Practice before a qualifying exam is essential, and can make a significant difference to your score. It is obvious that practice will help. It will mean that you make fewer mistakes and work more quickly against the often tight time constraints. It will ensure you are familiar with the test demands, and that you revise forgotten rules and develop a good test technique.

If passing is important to you, you should be prepared to make a major commitment in terms of setting time aside to practise during the weeks leading up to the test. You can be sure that other candidates will make such a commitment, so you risk coming a poor second if you do not. To maximize the benefits of practice you should undertake two types of exercise:

- Warm-up practice. You should practise in a relaxed situation, without time constraints, on questions which are similar to those described in the department's test. The aim is to realize the test demands and work out why you got a question wrong. This way you revise the competencies and build up confidence in your own abilities.

- Realistic test practice against the clock. Now practise on realistic questions against a strict time limit and in circumstances as similar to the test as you can manage. The aim is to get used to answering the questions under the pressure of time and to build up speed and accuracy.

Practise on as much material as you can obtain but restrict your practice to questions similar to the real thing.

Practice for the administrative grades

'I used this book to understand and appreciate what is required to pass the tests for ordinary entry. It's a must for anyone trying to get in.' (Reader review)

Considerable decentralization has taken place in recruitment to the Civil Service. In the 1990s uniform, nationwide procedures were applied in every department or agency. Today only selection for the Fast Stream is done through a national test, with departments and agencies adopting their own procedures for recruitment to all other grades. This said, most departments continue to use a recruitment process that broadly comprises three features – application sifting, tests and panel interviews – and there is still considerable similarity in the competencies examined across all departments and agencies.

Most vacancies will be advertised through government websites, local papers and job centres. More senior grades such as executive officers may be advertised on the public service day in the national press, for example the *Guardian* (on Wednesdays) and journals such as the *New Scientist*.

Your work as an administrator in the Civil Service is likely to consist of tasks such as dealing with customers, operating computer systems and updating records, financial administration, procurement, marketing or public relations.

If you join as an administrative assistant, you will be involved in general clerical duties and could be filing and looking after official papers and documents, or writing straightforward letters. You may also be involved in receiving and dispatching correspondence, photocopying and distributing documents, or answering and making telephone calls.

Responsibilities for administrative officers may include: preparing documentation in accordance with guidance, researching and collating information, updating computer data and maintaining accurate records, writing reports and the supervision of administrative assistants.

If you're already at middle or senior management level, then consider applying for a position as an executive officer. This role focuses on people management and duties such as co-ordinating large-scale clerical exercises, organizing training and assisting in business management.

Tests are often used in the recruitment to these grades; they may be online or you may be asked to sit a paper-and-pen version. If you have never taken a psychometric test before, then to get some idea of what to expect think back to the days of examinations, and in particular SATs (short-answer tests) at school. The qualifying exams for the Civil Service are almost certain to consist of multiple choice or short-answer questions, and you must compete for one of the places against other candidates.

If you are invited to attend a test centre you will face either a room set out as an examination hall with small desks, or banks of computer terminals, depending on whether you face a paper-and-pen or computer-administered version of the test. Other candidates are very likely to be present. In some instances there may be a lot of them. A test administrator will welcome you and explain the process. He or she will be following a prepared script, and will be happy to answer any questions, although the answers given may be rather brief or superficial. This is because the administrator is keen that all candidates (including those who attend on a different day and will not have heard your question) receive the same information and experience the same test conditions, so he or she will be reluctant to stray far from the script.

Whether you face a test online or at a test centre, if you suffer a disability that may affect your performance and means you require things to be organized in a different way, then contact the department or agency straight away.

The types of practice question in this chapter

The following questions are characteristic of the type used to recruit to the administrative grades described above. But check their relevance to the particular test that you face before you spend time working through the material. This chapter offers practice in the types of question listed below. The next chapter provides further questions under practice test conditions:

- handling data: the essentials (38 questions);
- quantitative reasoning (29 questions);
- data interpretation (34 questions);
- word swap (19 questions);
- missing words (21 questions);
- correct sentences (20 questions);
- following procedures (10 questions);
- speed and accuracy (23 questions).

To maximize the benefit of practice you may need more material than is contained in this volume. Sources of other suitable practice material in the Kogan Page testing series include:

- *The Numeracy Test Workbook*;
- *How to Pass Numeracy Tests*;

- *How to Pass Numerical Reasoning Tests: A Step by Step Approach to the Key Skills;*
- *The Ultimate Psychometric Test Book;*
- *How to Pass Verbal Tests;*
- *How to Pass Selection Tests.*

In some tests for the Civil Service you are allowed a calculator, but even so don't risk taking a real test unless you have revised your mental arithmetic. For this reason I have suggested that you do not use a calculator to answer the following questions (but by all means use one to check your answers or when trying to work out where you have gone wrong).

Handling data: the essentials

You should be able to answer these questions without a calculator in under 10 seconds. Once you manage that, you should practise some more until you can answer them in 5 seconds! So get practising. There is no better way than practice to improve your speed and accuracy in this key competency.

Try the following 38 questions.

1. Orlando is facing south. If he turns through one right angle anticlockwise, in which direction will he face?

    Answer: [   ]

2. Allegra is facing north and turns through three right angles in a clockwise direction. In what direction does she now face?

    Answer: [   ]

3. Greg turns through two right angles in a clockwise direction. He ends up facing south. In which direction was he originally facing?

    Answer: [   ]

4. David is lost. He set off this morning walking due west and from the sun's position can tell that he is now facing due east. He knows he made two right-angled turns. Can you tell if he turned clockwise or anticlockwise from the information given?

    Answer: [   ]

5. A store sells batteries for £3.00 for a pack of four. What is the cost of each battery?

    Answer: [   ]

6. A store sells batteries for £3.00 for a pack of four. How many batteries will you get for £21?

    Answer: [   ]

7. A shop sells batteries for £1.33 each. How much will four cost?

    Answer: [   ]

8. A shop sells batteries for £1.50. What is the cost of 12?

    Answer: [   ]

9.   A supermarket needs 48 till rolls for a usual Saturday's trading. The rolls come in packs of three. How many packs will the store use on a typical Saturday?

Answer: [   ]

10. Eggs are sold in boxes of six for £1.56. How much would 24 eggs cost?

Answer: [   ]

11. Eggs are sold in boxes of six for £1.56. How much would 20 eggs cost? (Assume that the store will split a box.)

Answer: [   ]

12. A medium-sized egg weighs 60 g. How much do six weigh?

Answer: [   ]

13. If six eggs weigh in total 300 g, how much would you expect four of them to weigh?

Answer: [   ]

14. Lola raised £132 for charity by giving sponsored Italian language lessons. She charges £12 a lesson, so how many lessons did she give?

Answer: [   ]

15. Hope was sponsored 30p for each length that she swam. She raised a total of £12.00. How many lengths did she manage to swim?

Answer: [   ]

16. A kilo of parmesan cheese costs £16.00. How much would a piece that weighed 550 g cost?

Answer: [   ]

17. 400 g of beans comprises 1,600 beans. How much does each bean weigh?

Answer: [   ]

18. Ten heaps each contains 37 individual beans, and each bean has an average weight of 0.3 g. How much do all the beans weigh (ie all the beans in all the heaps)?

Answer: [   ]

19. Douglas purchased 25 kilos of potatoes at 28p a kilo. How much did he spend?

Answer: [   ]

20. An electricity bill is calculated by a charge of 10.1p for each unit of power used. How much would the charge be if you had used 660 units?

Answer: [   ]

21. The tax on electricity charges of £ 48.00 is 5 per cent. How much tax will be added to the charge?

Answer: [   ]

22. 20 per cent of men responded positively when asked whether or not they hated Mondays. If the total survey comprised 60 men, how many responded positively to the question?

Answer: [   ]

23. At a bus terminus, one bus is scheduled to arrive every three minutes. How many should arrive during a four-hour shift?

Answer: [   ]

24. Ella counted 30 aeroplanes going over her house in a six-hour period. How many minutes separated each plane? (Assume the intervals were equal.)

Answer: [   ]

25. On the day of the train drivers' strike, 13 staff out of a workforce of 39 arrived at work late. What percentage of the workers were late that day?

Answer: [   ]

26. If this exercise comprised a total of 45 questions and you were allowed 10 seconds to attempt each, how long would the exercise last?

Answer: [   ]

27. Nine people ate at a restaurant and agreed to share the bill equally. The bill came to £202.50. How much did each have to contribute?

Answer: [   ]

28. You agreed to pay half the cost of a carpet for a room with an area of 4 square metres at a cost of £30 per square metre. What is the value of your contribution?

Answer: [   ]

29. You have agreed to a 12 per cent service charge on a bill of £112. How much extra will the cost be?

Answer:

30. Tax is levied at 17.5 per cent on the net cost of sales totalling £12,000. Will the tax be more than £2,000?

Answer:

31. What is 324 divided by 12?

Answer:

32. If tax is levied at 17.5 per cent, is it correct that £262,500 of tax would be payable on sales of one and a half million?

Answer:

33. The instructions on a bottle recommend that you mix the contents with water at a ratio of 1:5 (ie five times as much water). How much water should you add to 225 ml of the bottle's contents?

Answer:

34. If a train left at 11.35 am on a journey that normally takes 3 hours 20 minutes, but arrived 30 minutes late, what was its eventual time of arrival?

Answer:

35. If the sterling/euro exchange rate is 1:1.53, how many euros would you receive in exchange for £20?

Answer:

36. If an apartment in Venice was sold for 500,000 euros, would the vendor receive more or less than £320,000 if the sterling/euro exchange rate was 1:1.53?

Answer: [   ]

37. By how many would the pig population grow if a sow was to have a litter of nine, and each of her offspring was to grow up and also have a first litter of nine?

Answer: [   ]

38. In 2002 there were 530 secondary schools in Greater London. The government wanted to increase this total by 16 schools. What approximate percentage increase does this represent?

Answer: [   ]

Quantitative reasoning

Attempt these questions without a calculator. Indicate your answer by writing the letter of the correct answer, A–F, in the answer box. Practise until you are able to answer each in under 30 seconds. Twenty-nine examples are given.

1. If a dozen pens cost £1.20, how much do three and a half dozen cost?

   A £3.20   B £32   C £4.20   D £2.20   E £2.40   F £3.10

Answer: [   ]

2.   Two identical parcels weigh 0.5 kg. One parcel and a letter weigh 0.35 kg. How much do two letters weigh?

A 0.25 kg   B 0.1 kg   C 0.15 kg   D 0.2 kg   E 0.3 kg
F 0.5 kg

Answer: [   ]

3.   A company took advantage of a special offer and bought an overhead projector for one-third of its full price. How much was the discount?

A 25%   B 66.66%   C 60%   D 33.33%   E 30%
F 20%

Answer: [   ]

4.   In 2000, a company made a profit of £24,840. In 2001 the profit increased by one quarter. How much profit did the company make in 2001?

A £6,210   B £30,050   C £5,210   D £32,050
E £32,240   F £31,050

Answer: [   ]

5.   In March Rob made 64 calls from his mobile, and his bill for March was £16. In April Rob made 25 per cent fewer calls. How many calls did Rob make in April, and how much was his bill?

A 16 / £4   B 48 / £12   C 38 / £12   D 32 / £12
E 32 / £6   F 34 / £4

Answer: [   ]

6. The total business revenue for 2000 was £277,000. Staff wages were £67,000, overheads were £21,000 and production cost was £103,000. How much profit did the company make in 2000?

    A £262,000   B £87,000   C £98,000   D £86,000
    E £96,000   F £106,000

    Answer: [   ]

7. Mary is organizing transport for 150 conference attendees. If three coaches can accommodate 75 passengers, how many coaches should Mary hire?

    A 3   B 2   C 4   D 6   E 5   F 7

    Answer: [   ]

8. The total amount of money generated by ticket sales for a conference is £ 1,134.00. The conference hall can accommodate 126 people. Assuming they all bought a ticket and paid the same price, what was the price of a single ticket?

    A £9   B £11   C £8.50   D £10.50   E £7   F £8.50

    Answer: [   ]

9. Sophie works Monday to Friday. She leaves her house at 6.15 am to arrive at work at 7.45. It takes her just as long to get back home in the evening. How much time does she spend commuting per week?

    A 13 h   B 14.15 h   C 7.30 h   D 15 h   E 5 h   F 15.30 h

    Answer: [   ]

10. Last week Ann worked 2 h overtime, Fred worked 1.30 h overtime, Lisa worked 1 h overtime, Mary worked 2.30 h overtime and Bob worked 3 h overtime. How many hours overtime did they work on average?

    A 10 h   B 3 h   C 2.32 h   D 2.30 h   E 2 h   F 3.32 h

    Answer: [   ]

11. Phil is earning £70 per week and his wife Rose £80 per week. Phil receives a 5 per cent pay rise and Rose decides to work only part time, so she is earning 45 per cent less than before. How much is their new combined income per week?

    A £109.50   B £108.10   C £116.10   D £117.50
    E £110.00   F £197.50

    Answer: [   ]

12. A petty-cash box contains 7 × 50p coins, 18 × 20p coins, 33 × 10p coins, 12 × 5p coins and 15 × 2p coins. How much money in total is in the petty cash box?

    A £23.10   B £20.10   C £21.10   D £12.30   E £15.30
    F £11.30

    Answer: [   ]

13. 24 per cent of the staff working for a company are self-employed; the remainder are employed directly by the company. Of those directly employed, 18 per cent of the total staff work full time, while 29 members of staff are employed on a part-time basis. How many members of staff are self-employed?

    A 36   B 29   C 48   D 18   E 9   F 12

    Answer: [   ]

14. The total capital invested into a partnership is £70,000. Partner A invested 2.5 times more than partner B. How much money did partner B invest?

    A £25,000   B £50,000   C £28,000   D £20,000
    E £9,800   F £19,800

    Answer:

15. If one photocopier can produce 180 copies per hour, how many copies can two photocopiers produce in 25 minutes?

    A 125   B 175   C 150   D 145   E 75   F 200

    Answer:

16. Angela spends 7 h per day in the office and works five days per week. She spends 3/7 of her time typing letters. How much time does Angela spend typing letters per week?

    A 15 h   B 7.30 h   C 20 h   D 20.30 h   E 15.30 h
    F 12 h

    Answer:

17. A carpet-cleaning company charges £2.25 per sq m. How much would it cost to clean a wall-to-wall carpet in an office sized 12 m by 18.5 m?

    A £222   B £202   C £499.50   D £555   E £495
    F £495.50

    Answer:

18. Hasan earns £400 per week before tax. His tax is £64 per week. In percentage terms, how much tax is Hasan paying?

    A 25%   B 64%   C 17.5%   D 8%   E 12%   F 16%

    Answer:

19. An architect constructed a model of a shopping centre using a scale 1:2,000. If the model is 57.5 cm long, how long will the actual shopping centre be when built?

   A 11, 500 m   B 1,250 m   C 115 m   D 1,150 m
   E 115,000.00 m   F 125 m

   Answer: [   ]

20. In an office, the ratio of male to female workers is 1:3.5. If there are four male workers, how many females work in the office?

   A 10   B 12   C 14   D 8   E 18   F 13

   Answer: [   ]

21. Mojisola is taking a business trip to Italy. If the exchange rate for pounds sterling to euros is 1:1.6, and she needs €400 per day, how many pounds should she exchange for a four-day stay?

   A £857   B £750   C £849.50   D £1,000   E £600
   F £500

   Answer: [   ]

22. John earns £18,700 pa. Sarah earns £28,000 pa. How much is Mark earning pa if he earns 47 per cent less than John and Sarah together?

   A £24,751   B £20,959   C £18,959   D £21,959
   E £21,949   F £22,949

   Answer: [   ]

23. The profit for 1999 was £1,250. If the profit increases by 10 per cent each year, how much profit will be made in 2001?

   A £1,500   B £1,512.5   C £1,650   D £1,525
   E £15,125   F £1,652

   Answer: [   ]

24. The population in an area has a ratio of 3:7 young to old inhabitants. If a company wishes to reflect the same ratio among its 370 employees, how many of them should be old?

   A 259   B 111   C 255   D 198   E 220   F 225

   Answer: [   ]

25. To reach its annual target, a sales team has to achieve on average 150 sales per quarter. At the end of the third quarter the sales are averaging 137 per quarter. How many sales must the sales team achieve during the final quarter to reach the target?

   A 211   B 123   C 189   D 150   E 137   F 411

   Answer: [   ]

26. Susan earns £15,400 pa after paying 23 per cent tax. How much is her annual income before tax?

   A £20,000   B £17,220   C £24,780   D £15,376
   E £16,450   F £18,881

   Answer: [   ]

27. Company A employs twice as many people as Company B. Company C employs 25 per cent fewer people than Company A. If Company C employs 120, how many does Company B employ?

A 75   B 60   C 150   D 120   E 80   F 160

Answer: [   ]

28. The size of an office is 11 m by 12.5 m. How many carpet tiles sized 50 cm by 50 cm are required to cover the office floor, excluding the area underneath the filing cabinet? The base of the filing cabinet is 1.25 m by 80 cm.

A 568   B 546   C 548   D 136.5   E 188   F 176.5

Answer: [   ]

29. The budget for organizing a seminar is £3,700. Of this, 35 per cent is spent on hiring a venue. A quarter of the remainder is used to pay a speaker, while 2/3 is paid for transport to and from the venue. How much of the budget is left for refreshments? Round your answer to the nearest pound.

A £199   B £217   C £170   D £153   E £200   F £76

Answer: [   ]

Data interpretation

This type of test comprises tables or charts of information that you must interpret in order to answer the questions that follow. Thirty-four examples are provided. Indicate your answer by writing the letter of the correct answer, A–F, in the answer box.

Table 2.1   Acceptances for settlement in the UK: by category of acceptance

| | Thousands | | | |
	1985	1990	1995	2000
New Commonwealth				
Own right	4.1	2.4	1.7	1.6
Husbands	3.2	3.2	6.3	6.0
Wives	10.0	3.9	9.6	9.6
Children	10.7	3.2	4.5	4.5
Others	3.4	3.3	5.8	6.1
Total New Commonwealth	31.4	16.0	27.9	27.8
Rest of the world				
Own right	11.6	6.6	9.3	4.0
Husbands	3.4	6.1	5.4	4.9
Wives	6.8	4.8	3.7	9.0
Children	3.7	2.9	3.1	3.9
Others	2.3	3.6	4.7	3.2
Total rest of the world	27.8	24.0	26.2	25.0
Total acceptances	59.2	40.0	54.1	52.6

1.   How many people settled in the UK in 2000?

A 25,000   B 27,000   C 48,000   D 52,600   E 54,000
F 59,200

Answer:

2. In which year were acceptances from the New Commonwealth proportionally less than from the rest of the world?

   A 1985   B 1990   C 1995   D 2000   E None
   F Information not available

   Answer: [   ]

3. In 1995 which category was the least accepted overall?

   A Own right   B Husbands   C Wives   D Children
   E Others   F None

   Answer: [   ]

4. How many more children from the rest of the world were accepted in 2000 than in 1985?

   A 0   B 20   C 200   D 800   E 2,000   F 8,000

   Answer: [   ]

5. What percentage of total acceptances in 1990 were from the New Commonwealth?

   A 20%   B 40%   C 60%   D 70%   E 80%   F 90%

   Answer: [   ]

Table 2.2 All aboard the ferry: Summer 2002 timetable*

Pier Head depart	Seaway arrive/depart	Riverside arrive/depart	Pier Head arrive	Fare (£)
10.00 am	10.30 am	10.40 am	10.50 am	2.20
11.00 am	11.30 am	11.40 am	11.50 am	2.20
12.00 pm	12.30 pm	12.40 pm	12.50 pm	2.20
1.00 pm	1.30 pm	1.40 pm	1.50 pm	2.20
2.00 pm	2.30 pm	2.40 pm	2.50 pm	2.20
3.00 pm	3.30 pm	3.40 pm	3.50 pm	2.20
4.15 pm	4.25 pm	4.35 pm	4.45 pm	1.15
4.45 pm	4.55 pm	5.05 pm	5.15 pm	1.15
5.15 pm	5.25 pm	5.35 pm	5.45 pm	1.15
5.45 pm	5.55 pm	6.05 pm	6.15 pm	1.15

* Between 10.00 am and 3.00 pm the ferry makes a scenic round trip, leaving Pier Head each hour on the hour

6.   How long is the scenic cruise?

   A 30 minutes   B 50 minutes   C 1 hour
   D 5 hours 50 minutes   E 6 hours   F 6 hours 15 minutes

   Answer: [   ]

7.   What time does the 1.00 pm ferry from Pier Head arrive at Riverside?

   A 1.30 pm   B 1.40 pm   C 1.50 pm   D 2.00 pm
   E 2.40 pm   F 3.00 pm

   Answer: [   ]

8.   What is the longest time the ferry waits at Pier Head?

   A 5 minutes   B 10 minutes   C 15 minutes
   D 20 minutes   E 25 minutes   F 30 minutes

   Answer: [   ]

9.   A party of 50 tourists board the 2.00 pm scenic cruise. How much in total do they pay for this tour?

A £57.50   B £65.00   C £100.00   D £110.00
E £125.00   F £140.00

Answer: [   ]

10. At 4.00 pm a tanker anchors off Seaway. This results in a 15-minute delay between Seaway and Riverside on all journeys from then on. What time does the ferry finally finish at Pier Head that day?

A 5.00 pm   B 5.15 pm   C 6.15 pm   D 6.45 pm
E 7.15 pm   F Insufficient information

Answer: [   ]

Delilah Smythe is baking cakes, but she has a gas oven and the recipe only gives temperatures in °C. She therefore looks up her handy conversion table.

Table 2.3   Conversion table

| Gas mark | Oven temperatures | |
	°F	°C
1	275	140
2	300	150
3	325	170
4	350	180
5	375	190
6	400	200
7	425	220
8	450	230
9	475	240

11. The recipe says, 'Bake the cakes at 180°C for 20–25 minutes until brown on top'. What Gas Mark should Delilah use?

A 1   B 2   C 3   D 4   E 5   F 6

Answer: [   ]

12. At Gas Marks 2 and 6, what is the difference between the readings in °F and °C?

A x1   B x2   C x3   D x4   E x5   F x6

Answer: [   ]

13. What is the range in temperature, measured in °F, between Gas Marks 3 and 9?

A 70°F   B 100°F   C 125°F   D 150°F   E 175°F
F 200°F

Answer: [   ]

14. Delilah uses a thermometer to check the temperature of her oven at the various Gas Marks and finds that Gas Mark 6 is 5 per cent higher than it should be. What temperature, in °C, does the thermometer read?

A 190°C   B 200°C   C 210°C   D 220°C   E 230°C
F 240°C

Answer: [   ]

The Stephenson family love to shop. The family of five easily spends over £300 each week at Sainsways on groceries. Here is part of their till receipt for one week in March:

```
CUCUMBER WHOLE              0.59 g
ORGANIC ORANGES             1.49 g
S GREENS                    0.75 g
S P/NUT/BUT SMTH            1.99
S P/NUT/BUT SMTH            1.99
* MULTISAVE *              -1.99
S SATSUMA LARGE             1.79 g
PURE ORANGE JUICEX1LTR      0.99
S SOAP MULTIPACK            1.75
S SATSUMA LARGE             1.79 g
* MULTISAVE *              -1.79
S TOOTHPASTE                0.88
0.745 kg @ £2.49 / kg
S GRAPES WHT S/LESS         1.86 g
**** TOT                  302.60

16/03/02 16.07
```

Figure 2.1   Till receipt

15. How much is 1 litre of pure orange juice?

    A £0.99   B £1.49   C £1.75   D £1.79   E £1.99
    F Information not supplied

    Answer: [   ]

16. How much have the Stephenson family saved on multisaves?

    A £1.79   B £1.99   C £2.67   D £3.78   E £4.02
    F £4.52

    Answer: [   ]

17. How much did the Stephenson family spend on groceries (g)?

    A £0.56 B £1.42 C £3.65 D £5.64 E £6.48
    F £8.27

    Answer: [   ]

18. Mrs Stephenson has collected 250 discount points on her loyalty card, worth 10 per cent of the total bill. How much does she save?

    A £20.50 B £25.00 C £30.26 D £33.60 E £40.62
    F £40.88

    Answer: [   ]

Table 2.4 Holiday entitlement

Name	Annual holiday entitlement	Carry-over from the previous year	Total numbers of days taken to date	Days remaining
M. Adams	23	0	1.5	21.5
S. Brown	23	−1	11	?
H. Evans	27	2	5	?
H. Hasan	26	0	5	?
A. Milic	23	−1.5	8	?

19. From the table above, how many more days holiday can S. Brown take in the current year?

    A 22 B 24 C 11 D 21 E 19 F 18

    Answer: [   ]

20. Employees are given 23 days holiday per year during the first two years of service and then an extra half day for every six months of service. How many years has H. Hasan been with the company?

A 4   B 6   C 4.5   D 5   E 3.5   F 5.5

Answer: [   ]

21. A. Milic earns £300 per week. If she decides to resign and work throughout her notice period without taking any more holiday, how much holiday pay will she be entitled to? Assume that her last day of employment coincides with the end of the year for holiday entitlement purposes.

A £900   B £22.22   C £810   D £620   E £720   F £600

Answer: [   ]

22. If S. Brown wants to go away for 15 days, how many days unpaid leave should he take in addition to his holiday entitlement?

A 5   B 3   C 0   D 1   E 4   F 2

Answer: [   ]

Table 2.5 shows the realized sales of a mobile phone package priced at £49, and the commission earned per sale.

Table 2.5   Mobile phone package sales

Name	Target in units	Units sold	Commission (%)	Total (%)	Earnings
S. Amed	25	24	3	35.28	
B. Fay	25	31	3	?	
S. Grant	25	28	3	41.16	
I. Jones	25	21	3	30.87	
O. Khann	25	26	3	38.22	
A. Lewis	25	26	3	38.22	

23. From the table calculate the total commission earned by B. Fay.

A £28.30   B £93.00   C £45.57   D £36.75   E £55.75   F £28.00

Answer: [ ]

24. On average, how many units did each salesperson sell during the period?

A 26   B 22   C 21   D 29   E 27   F 28

Answer: [ ]

25. If the company decided to increase the commission to 5 per cent for every unit sold above the target, how much commission would S. Grant earn?

A £52.30   B £60   C £37.75   D £53.17   E £44.10   F £43.17

Answer: [ ]

26. What percentage of employees reached the target?

A 25%   B 30%   C 60%   D 70%   E 66.6%   F 33.3%

Answer: [ ]

Table 2.6 shows the net total (income after tax) generated by the products.

Table 2.6   Net total generated by products

Product	Number of units (in 000s)	Cost of raw material per unit (£)	Manufacturing cost per unit (£)	Total cost per unit (£)	Sales price per unit (£)	Total sales revenue (£) (sales price – total cost x number of units)
A	21.5	3.75	2	5.75	7.5	37,625.00
B	18	2.19	3.17	5.36	6.25	1,602.00
C	7	8.70	4.2	12.90	13.4	3,500.00
D	11.75	0.57	4.8	5.37	7.99	?
E	12.8	1.18	0.27	1.45	4.5	39,040.00
F	9.25	4.3	1.5	5.8	6.25	4,162.50
Total Profit (–23%)	80.3	20.69	15.94	36.63	45.89	743,578.00

27. From the table, calculate which product is the most profitable.

    A F   B D   C E   D A   E C   F B

    Answer: [   ]

28. If the manufacturing cost were reduced by 50 per cent, what would be the total sales revenue for product A?

    A £60,700   B £49,125   C £57,755   D £59,125
    E £48,950   F £66,789

    Answer: [   ]

29. Calculate the total sales revenue for product D.

    A £40,500   B £30,785   C £30,885   D £45,125
    E £33,600   F £30,780

    Answer: _____

30. Assuming that the tax is 23 per cent, calculate the total profit for the period.

    A £572,555.06   B £57,255.56   C £171,022.94
    D £17,122.94   E £743,250.00   F £74,325.00

    Answer: _____

Table 2.7   Average temperatures in °C

Year	1st quarter	2nd quarter	3rd quarter	4th quarter
1996	1	12.5	23	2
1997	2	11	22	4
1998	−1	13.5	24	3.5
1999	0	10	21.5	4
2000	1.5	15.5	23	2
2001	2	14.5	25	?

31. From Table 2.7, what was the average temperature in 1999?

    A 8.9°C   B 9°C   C 8.8°C   D 11.8°C   E 11.7°C
    F 10.7°C

    Answer: _____

32. Calculate the net change in temperature between the first and fourth quarters for 1998.

    A 2.5°C   B 4.5C°   C 3.5°C   D 2.5°C   E −4°C
    F −4.5°C

    Answer: _____

33. In what year was the greatest change in temperature between the first and third quarters?

    A 1996   B 1997   C 1998   D 1999   E 2000   F 2001

    Answer:

34. If the average temperature in 2000 was the same as in 2001, what was the temperature in the final quarter in 2001?

    A 2   B 2.5   C 1.5   D 1   E 5   F 0.5

    Answer:

Word swap

Each question comprises a sentence in which two words need to be interchanged to make it read sensibly. Only swap two words, so that one replaces the other. This means that one word must be placed where you have taken the other. Try the following 19 examples.

1. A loss of muscle movement is accompanied by rapid tone of the eyes.

    Answer:

2. Sometimes these remedies can result remarkably quickly, with a positive work occurring in a matter of hours.

    Answer:

3. Completely safe, it is made from artificial ingredients, with no natural colours, flavours or preservatives.

    Answer:

4. Over the centuries and of these properties have been sold some other properties purchased.

Answer: [   ]

5. Only the small doorway in the remain on the ground floor and a similar doorway on the northern wall of the gallery recess today.

Answer: [   ]

6. They take most day as it comes and work very hard to make the each of it.

Answer: [   ]

7. Perhaps the greatest advantage to the constant ability is see two sides to every story.

Answer: [   ]

8. It's true they have an enthusiastic style for information and a bubbly hunger of expression.

Answer: [   ]

9. The national minimum wage is over £4.20 an hour for workers aged 22 years or now.

Answer: [   ]

10. How thrilling to camp out in the jungle surrounded of the incredible sounds by the equatorial night.

Answer: [   ]

11. Many people believe that we should eat our national produce more and only respect fruit and vegetables that are in season.

Answer: [   ]

12. If your dog does kill a rabbit it may be necessary for you to put the rabbit out of its misery and catch it yourself.

Answer: [   ]

13. A few golfers rake to forget the sand in the bunker after their shot, which can cause problems for the next person.

Answer: [   ]

14. The most popular numerous orange is the Seville, a thinned-skinned orange-red fruit, with acid, deep yellow flesh and bitter pips.

Answer: [   ]

15. The adaptable alphabet is the most highly developed, convenient and the most easily Roman system of writing.

Answer: [   ]

16. A damp-proof course is a layer of inserted material impervious in the bottom of a house wall about 20 cm above ground level.

Answer: [   ]

17. There are few things as idyllic as opening up the picnic basket in an irritating spot only to find the tin/bottle opener is back on the kitchen table.

Answer: ☐

18. The known benefits of raw fish, soya beans and green tea have long been health to the Japanese.

Answer: ☐

19. It would be unwise to venture out of the house during springtime in England about an umbrella without one's person.

Answer: ☐

Missing words

In each of the sentences below, two words are missing. Beneath the sentence are four groups of two words each. One group has the two words in the order in which they fall in the sentence. It is your task to identify which are the correct pairings from the sound or look-alike alternatives.

Indicate your answer by writing the letters of the correct pair, A–D, in the answer box. Try the following 21 examples.

1. To _____ any sort of change, the proposed legislation must have an _____ that is clearly felt by the community.

A	B	C	D
affect	effect	aphect	ephect
effect	effect	ephect	aphect

Answer: ☐

2.   He was _____ upon the goodwill of his father; he was after all his sole _____.

A	B	C	D
depandent	dependant	dependent	deapendent
depandant	dependent	dependant	deapandant

Answer: [   ]

3.   He _____ with pleasure his _____ to fish in the Loch.

A	B	C	D
excepted	accepted	excepted	accepted
license	licence	licence	license

Answer: [   ]

4.   It will be on David's _____ if Lucy does not remain _____ throughout the night.

A	B	C	D
concience	conscience	conscience	concience
conscious	conscious	consious	conscious

Answer: [   ]

5.   The girl _____ a glass out of the _____ window.

A	B	C	D
threw	through	threw	though
rear	rare	reer	wrear

Answer: [   ]

6. The cutter he was going to use to _____ the tree had a blueish _____ to it.

A	B	C	D
hugh	hew	hue	huw
hue	hue	hew	hugh

Answer: [   ]

7. Honesty was Helen's first _____ when she became _____ of the school.

A	B	C	D
princepal	princaple	principle	principal
princaple	principle	principal	principal

Answer: [   ]

8. It is common _____ to _____ to the queen as she passes.

A	B	C	D
courtesy	curtesy	courtesey	curtesey
curtsy	quertsey	courtsey	qurtsey

Answer: [   ]

9. The raid on the _____ resulted in _____ action being taken.

A	B	C	D
dispensery	dispansary	disspensary	disspensery
disciplinery	disciplinary	disiplinary	disiplinery

Answer: [   ]

10. She kept a _____ of artefacts for when the _____ of
    pilgrims came by.

A	B	C	D
horde	hord	hoard	whord
hoarde	herd	horde	wherd

    Answer: [   ]

11. What you can do to make your cut _____ last even
    longer is to dip the cut ends in _____ before putting
    them in water.

A	B	C	D
flours	fluers	flowers	flouers
flower	flouer	flour	fluer

    Answer: [   ]

12. Take a _____ of fruit and _____ the skin with a pin.

A	B	C	D
peice	piece	peace	piece
pearce	peirce	peirse	pierce

    Answer: [   ]

13. I had to _____ the authorities she was too _____ to
    travel.

A	B	C	D
informe	inform	infourm	informn
inferm	infirm	inferme	infirmn

    Answer: [   ]

14. It was the _____ of such a musician to _____ for five
    hours each day.

A	B	C	D
practise	practice	practisce	practicse
practice	practise	practicse	practisce

    Answer: [   ]

15. It was while the van was _____ at the traffic lights that
    the _____ on board was stolen.

A	B	C	D
stationary	stationery	stationray	stationarey
stationery	stationary	stationrey	stationeray

    Answer: [   ]

16. On the back of the _____ was a _____ for
    marmalade.

A	B	C	D
rescite	resept	reciept	receipt
resepy	recipy	receipe	recipe

    Answer: [   ]

17. For the best results you must do the _____ _____
    upon getting up.

A	B	C	D
excersises	exersises	excercises	exercises
imediately	immidiately	immedietely	immediately

    Answer: [   ]

18. As a _____ you are not allowed to _____ the machine.

A	B	C	D
miner	minor	miener	mienor
opporate	operate	oparate	operate

Answer: [   ]

19. These _____ took those other _____ books by mistake.

A	B	C	D
boys	bouys	boy's	boys'
boys'	bouy's	boys	boy's

Answer: [   ]

20. _____ most unusual for the dog to refuse _____ bone like that.

A	B	C	D
its	it's	its'	it
it's	its	it	its'

Answer: [   ]

21. Even when using a _____ line the wall does not look _____.

A	B	C	D
plum	plumb	plump	plumn
strait	straight	strate	streight

Answer: [   ]

Correct sentences

Identify which of the options is correct in terms of grammar, spelling and punctuation. Below you will find 20 examples of this type of question. Indicate your answer by writing the letter of the correct sentence, a)–d), in the answer box.

1. a) If you're looking for an evening out this month, there are big offers on musicals and pop concerts.
   b) If you're looking for an evening out this month, there is big offers on musicals and pop concerts.
   c) If your looking for an evening out this month, there are big offers on musicals and pop concerts.
   d) None of these.

Answer: [   ]

2. a) The consumer is protected from exploitation by a given seller by the existence of other seller's he can buy from.
   b) The consumer is protected from exploitation by a given seller by the existence of other sellers from whom he can buy.
   c) The consumer are protected from exploitation by a given seller by the existence of other sellers from whom he can buy.
   d) None of these.

Answer: [   ]

3. a) All mammal's produce eggs within which their young develop.
   b) All mammal's produce eggs which their young develop in.
   c) All mammals produce eggs within which their young develop.
   d) None of these.

Answer: [   ]

4. a) There are maps and travel books available for most of England's towns and cities.
   b) There is maps and travel books available for most of England's towns and cities.
   c) Maps and travel books is available for most of England's Towns and Cities.
   d) None of these.

   Answer: [   ]

5. a) Further information will be given to you when you visited the head office.
   b) Further information was given to you when you visit the head office.
   c) Further information will be given to you when you visit the head office.
   d) None of these.

   Answer: [   ]

6. a) She married again, which surprised everybody who knew her.
   b) She married again, what surprised everybody who knew her.
   c) She married again, that surprised everybody whom knew her.
   d) None of these.

   Answer: [   ]

7. a) There are a wide selection of gifts available, all of which can be ordered by post or online.
    b) There is a wide selection of gifts available, all of which can be ordered by post online.
    c) There is a wide selection of gifts available, all of which will be ordered by post or online.
    d) None of these.

Answer: [   ]

8. a) At that moment, I wished I had gone to the same university as John.
    b) At that moment, I wished I was gone to the same university as John.
    c) At that moment, I wished I had gone to the same university as John did.
    d) None of these.

Answer: [   ]

9. a) When I go to university I'll not have no time for reading novels.
    b) When I go to university I won't have no time for reading novels.
    c) When I go to university I will have no time for reading novels.
    d) None of these.

Answer: [   ]

10. a) The coach was expecting great things off the team this season.
    b) The coach was expecting great things of the team this season.
    c) The coach were expecting great things of the team this season.
    d) None of these.

    Answer: [   ]

11. a) Whenever a new book comes out she is the first to buy a copy.
    b) Whenever a new book comes out she are the first to buy a copy.
    c) Whenever a new book comes out she is the first too buy a copy.
    d) None of these.

    Answer: [   ]

12. a) There are the promise of a more secure future for those who save on a regular basis.
    b) There is the promise of a more secure future for those who save on a regular basis.
    c) Their is the promise of a more secure future for those who saved on a regular basis.
    d) None of these.

    Answer: [   ]

13. a) If the customer does return the goods, you must check them before you gave a refund.
    b) If the customer did return the goods, you must ensure you check them before giving a refund.
    c) If the customer should return the goods, you must ensure you check them before giving a refund.
    d) None of the above.

Answer:

14. a) There's places where that kind of behaviour is unacceptable.
    b) There are places where that kind of behaviour is unacceptable.
    c) There's place's where that kind of behaviour is unacceptable.
    d) None of these.

Answer:

15. a) This borough is very good about providing bins for recycling metal, plastic, glass and paper.
    b) This borough are very good about providing bins for recycling metal, plastic, glass and paper.
    c) This borough is very good while providing bins for recycling metal, plastic, glass and paper.
    d) None of these.

Answer:

16. a) One of the most important notes on the piano are Middle C.
   b) One of the most important note's on the piano is Middle C.
   c) One of the most important notes on the piano is Middle C.
   d) None of these.

Answer: [   ]

17. a) Once Simon got angry it takes a long while for him to calm down.
   b) Once Simon gets angry it takes a long while for him to calm down.
   c) Once Simon gets angry it took a long while for him to calm down.
   d) None of these.

Answer: [   ]

18. a) We pitched our tent on the bank of the river Stour, near where it joins the Avon.
   b) We pitched our tent on the bank of the river Stour, near where it joined the Avon.
   c) We pitched our tent on the bank of the river Stour, near where it is joining the Avon.
   d) None of these.

Answer: [   ]

19. a) They was walking along the beach all day yesterday and they will be walking along the cliff all day tomorrow.
    b) They were walking along the beach all day yesterday and they were walking along the cliff all day tomorrow.
    c) They were walking along the beach all day yesterday and they will be walking along the cliff all day tomorrow.
    d) None of these.

Answer: [   ]

20. a) It was Galileo who discovered that Jupiter has moons.
    b) It was Galileo whom discovered that Jupiter had moons.
    c) It's Galileo who discovered that Jupiter had moons.
    d) None of these.

Answer: [   ]

Following procedures

This exercise measures your ability to follow explicit rules and interpret given information.

You are presented with a choice of 10 possible answers from which you must select the correct one(s). Please note that some of the practice questions require more than one suggested answer to be marked as correct. Indicate your answer by writing the letter(s) of the correct answer(s), A–J, in the answer box.

A credit management process

The flow chart below (Figure 2.2) illustrates the key points of the process.

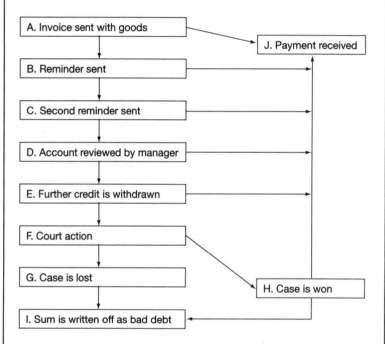

Figure 2.2

Rules governing the credit process

1. Invoices are sent out with goods and state that the company operates a strict 20-day credit facility from the date of invoice.
2. The first reminder is sent out 14 days after the goods. If payment is still not received, the second reminder is sent after a further 10 days.

3. Account reviews are held 17 days after the issuing of
    the second reminder.
4. In cases when the sum owed exceeds £100 and
    payment is not received within 20 days from the date
    of the account review, court action is instigated.
5. If the court case is lost, the amount is written off as a
    bad debt.
6. Without exception, credit facilities are withdrawn
    when the court action is initiated or when any sum
    becomes more than 60 days overdue.

Questions

1. Payment was received 22 working days after the date of
    invoice. What stage of the credit process would have last
    been implemented?

    A   B   C   D   E   F   G   H   I   J

    Answer: [   ]

2. Court action has had to be initiated against a creditor.
    What would have been the action taken immediately prior
    to this?

    A   B   C   D   E   F   G   H   I   J

    Answer: [   ]

3. A creditor has owed £98 for almost two months. What
    action should be taken?

    A   B   C   D   E   F   G   H   I   J

    Answer: [   ]

4. The average time taken for payment to be received is 39 working days from the invoice date. What stage of the process would next be initiated if payment was not received by then?

    A   B   C   D   E   F   G   H   I   J

    Answer: [   ]

5. Identify which stages could precede a debt being written off as bad.

    A   B   C   D   E   F   G   H   I   J

    Answer: [   ]

6. A payment has still not been received after 30 days. What action could be taken?

    A   B   C   D   E   F   G   H   I   J

    Answer: [   ]

7. What are the possible outcomes from court action?

    A   B   C   D   E   F   G   H   I   J

    Answer: [   ]

8. 20 days have passed since a case review. The sum outstanding is £120. What action should be taken?

    A   B   C   D   E   F   G   H   I   J

    Answer: [   ]

9. What actions can an account manager recommend?

    A   B   C   D   E   F   G   H   I   J

    Answer: [   ]

10. Since the date of the invoice 41 days have passed. What action is due to be taken?

A   B   C   D   E   F   G   H   I   J

Answer: [   ]

Speed and accuracy

The following speed and accuracy questions require you to compare sets of numbers or letters arranged in pairs, one on the left, the other on the right. Each set consists of four pairs, and you have to indicate how many of them are identical. You are offered five possible answers: all four (are identical), three pairs, two pairs, one pair or none. Indicate your answer by writing the letter of the correct answer, A–E, in the answer box.

1.   45981   45981
     xsbaa   xssa
     kiyhq   kiyhq
     21213   21213

     A All 4   B 3 pairs   C 2 pairs   D 1 pair   E None

                  Answer: [   ]

2.   qwdfk   wqdfk
     33601   33611
     15380   15580
     50179   97150

     A All 4   B 3 pairs   C 2 pairs   D 1 pair   E None

                  Answer: [   ]

3. hjwep   hjwep
    ffthm   ftthm
    abelo   abelo
    mwwgr   mnwgr

    A All 4   B 3 pairs   C 2 pairs   D 1 pair   E None

                    Answer:

4. 58392   53892
    dmhmi   dmdmi
    bdbdv   dbdbv
    illia   ilila

    A All 4   B 3 pairs   C 2 pairs   D 1 pair   E None

                    Answer:

5. zxasw   zxasw
    74893   74893
    17204   12704
    01010   01020

    A All 4   B 3 pairs   C 2 pairs   D 1 pair   E None

                    Answer:

6. bgdth   gbdth
    zakiv   zakii
    45000   54001
    45001   45000

    A All 4   B 3 pairs   C 2 pairs   D 1 pair   E None

                    Answer:

7.   sopme   soome
      soppq   soppq
      04517   04518
      49872   49872

      A All 4   B 3 pairs   C 2 pairs   D 1 pair   E None

                        Answer:

8.   mmhhi   mmhhh
      99933   33399
      fffrr   ffrr
      nhqir   nhqir

      A All 4   B 3 pairs   C 2 pairs   D 1 pair   E None

                        Answer:

9.   nxruy   nxruy
      qqasw   qqasw
      93462   93462
      ntyue   nteyu

      A All 4   B 3 pairs   C 2 pairs   D 1 pair   E None

                        Answer:

10.   15795   15795
      48957   48957
      25846   25864
      35745   35754

      A All 4   B 3 pairs   C 2 pairs   D 1 pair   E None

                        Answer:

11. ilop   kliop
     kopli   kploi
     poilk   polik
     oolip   ollip

     A All 4   B 3 pairs   C 2 pairs   D 1 pair   E None

                      Answer: [   ]

12. vfrtg   fgtrv
     gfrtv   gfrtv
     frtgv   frtgv
     gfrtf   rtfgt

     A All 4   B 3 pairs   C 2 pairs   D 1 pair   E None

                      Answer: [   ]

13. 20250   25052
     0425   0425
     65658   65658
     20052   20052

     A All 4   B 3 pairs   C 2 pairs   D 1 pair   E None

                      Answer: [   ]

14. blgos   blgos
     werqw   werqw
     14584   14584
     36526   36526

     A All 4   B 3 pairs   C 2 pairs   D 1 pair   E None

                      Answer: [   ]

15. 07078   07078
    asdfg   asdfg
    gfdsa   gfdsa
    03256   03256

    A All 4   B 3 pairs   C 2 pairs   D 1 pair   E None

    Answer:

16. wuyoi   wuyoi
    30057   30057
    dflkk   dflkk
    45008   45008

    A All 4   B 3 pairs   C 2 pairs   D 1 pair   E None

    Answer:

17. 49057   49057
    00558   00558
    asiore   asoire
    nheppo   nheppo

    A All 4   B 3 pairs   C 2 pairs   D 1 pair   E None

    Answer:

18. 4584584   4584584
    32658   32658
    500505   500505
    054585   0548458

    A All 4   B 3 pairs   C 2 pairs   D 1 pair   E None

    Answer:

19. gpr ty   gprty
     druowff   druuowff
     foluaw   foluaw
     brtrt   brtrt

     A All 4   B 3 pairs   C 2 pairs   D 1 pair   E None

     Answer: [   ]

20. 137946   137946
     438679   438679
     402794   4022794
     4586003   4586603

     A All 4   B 3 pairs   C 2 pairs   D 1 pair   E None

     Answer: [   ]

21. df er ty s   df er ty s
     fgtyoui   fgtyuoi
     cdf gtyg   cdfgtyy
     mmyyeeq   mmyyyeq

     A All 4   B 3 pairs   C 2 pairs   D 1 pair   E None

     Answer: [   ]

22. fdfre gt   fdre gg
     25 87 5   25 87 5
     bru ew   bru ee
     1579 587   1597 587

     A All 4   B 3 pairs   C 2 pairs   D 1 pair   E None

     Answer: [   ]

23. kuyjkrr   kuyjkrr
     qwqwreee   qwqwreeee
     nwkyiunn   nmkyiunn
     vetuyooi   vetyuooi

     A All 4   B 3 pairs   C 2 pairs   D 1 pair   E None

                              Answer: [   ]

Practice tests for the administrative grades

'You need to buy this book for all those extra questions.'
(Reader review)

The questions in this chapter have been arranged as practice tests with recommended time limits. The tests are realistic in terms of the question types and, most importantly, in terms of the sheer hard work and extended concentration required to do well in them. Develop these skills and they will serve you well in every psychometric test you take.

Use this chapter to practise under realistic test-like conditions. You should aim to develop a winning exam technique and to improve the rate at which you can answer the questions while not making too many mistakes. With this sort of practice your confidence in your abilities will soon increase, as will your mental stamina and agility. Practise getting your time management right. Do not spend too long on any single question; if you really can't answer one, then use educated guessing. This involves looking at the suggested answers and trying to rule out some as wrong, then guessing from the remaining options. Use any time at the end to check your answers. Realize that doing well in a test is not only down to your intelligence but also requires you to try your very best. So really go for it.

After each test, review the answers and explanations provided. Pay particular attention to any questions that you got wrong. Then take the next test. To make the test seem even more realistic, stick strictly to the suggested time limit and work without interruption or disturbance.

Our minds are wonderful things but prone to be a bit lazy. We can so easily convince ourselves that we have learnt something when in fact we have not. The only way to tell if we really have mastered something is to test ourselves.

Practice test 1: quantitative reasoning

This test consists of 30 questions. Allow yourself 20 minutes to complete it.

Set a stopwatch or the stopwatch function on a mobile phone, and stick strictly to the recommended time limit.

Be sure to revise your mental arithmetic before you sit a real test of quantitative reasoning. You may well be allowed to use a calculator in this type of test, so if you wish to use one in these practice tests, then do so, but sparingly. You still need to be sure of your mental arithmetic because then you will be better placed to see any error you might have made with the calculator. Moreover, you can often answer the questions faster if you do not have to check each calculation. Beware also if you are applying for lots of jobs, as you may well come up against a test in which a calculator is not allowed.

Select one answer from the suggested list. Indicate your answer by writing the letter of the correct answer in the answer box. Scrap paper is useful to help with any calculations.

Do not turn the page until you are ready to begin. Keep going until you have completed the last question or run out of time.

Quantitative reasoning

1. A secretary is posting 11 letters to clients. She is sending seven letters by first-class post at 27p per letter. The remaining four letters she is sending by second-class post at 19p per letter. How much postage is being paid for all 11 letters?

    A £2.77   B £1.27   C £1.76   D £2.41   E £2.56   F £2.65

    Answer:

2. A delivery was due to arrive at 14.45 but was 27 minutes late. At what time did it arrive?

    A 15.07   B 15.05   C 15.22   D 15.12   E 15.42   F 15.02

    Answer:

3. Ann deposits £1,000.00 in her savings account. The interest rate on her savings is 5 per cent. How long is it before Ann has earned £157 of interest?

    A 2.5 years   B 3.5 years   C 4 years   D 1.5 years   E 1 year
    F 3 years

    Answer:

4. A company purchased a new PC for £800. The depreciation rate (decrease in value) is 40 per cent for the first year and 25 per cent of the depreciated sum for every following year. What is the value of the PC at the end of the third year?

    A £48   B £240   C £270   D £280   E £230   F £58

    Answer:

5. An office junior can type 30 wpm. If he types steadily for 30 minutes, how many words will he type?

    A 90   B 600   C 60   D 120   E 800   F 900

    Answer:

6. An accountant has worked for a company for four months. His holiday allowance is 1.25 days per month in service. How many holiday days is the accountant entitled to after four months' service?

    A 4.25 days   B 6 days   C 5.5 days   D 3 days   E 5 days
    F 2 days

    Answer: [   ]

7. Petra is ordering stationery. She orders two boxes of staples for £1.75 each and five large notebooks for £1.15 each. All these prices are shown before VAT (17.5 per cent). How much will the total be including VAT?

    A £10.45   B £9.45   C £9.75   D £10.87   E £11.75
    F £9.45

    Answer: [   ]

8. A company manufactures small, medium and large buttons at the ratio of 1:5:3. If in 2001 the total of buttons manufactured was 18,900, how many of them were large?

    A 2,100   B 6,300   C 10,500   D 1,300   E 13,600
    F 6,800

    Answer: [   ]

9. A parcel weighing 1 kg costs £3.50 to post. If prices are proportional to weight, how much would it cost to post a parcel that weighs 200 g?

    A £1.75   B £1.25   C £0.75   D £0.70   E £1.15   F £0.89

    Answer: [   ]

10. A meeting is scheduled to start at 2:45 pm and last for 1 h 30 min. The trip from the office to the meeting venue takes 45 min. If Barbara is to attend the meeting, how long will she be away from the office?

A 3 h   B 2 h 45 min   C 3 h 15 min   D 4 h   E 2 h 30 min
F 3 h 45 min

Answer:

11. A company decides to buy corporate membership for its employees at the local gym. The gym is offering 20 per cent discount on all corporate memberships. How many members of staff should join for the company to receive the equivalent of two free memberships?

A 5   B 12   C 8   D 10   E 20   F 15

Answer:

12. With an offer buy-one-get-one-free, what percentage is saved?

A 25%   B 33%   C 50%   D 20%   E 35%   F 75%

Answer:

13. The total postage cost for two parcels of different weight is £3.40. If the weight ratio is 2:2.3, calculate the postage for the heavier parcel.

A £1.57   B £2.10   C £1.82   D £1.90   E £2.18   F £2.40

Answer:

14. Attendee A and attendee B are arriving for the same meeting from different locations. Attendee A is travelling at 47 mph over the distance of 38 miles. Attendee B is travelling at 38 mph over 29 miles. If they start their journeys at the same time, what will be the time gap between their arrivals? Round your answer up to a full minute.

    A 5 mins   B 3 mins   C 2 mins   D 7 mins   E 8 mins   F 4 mins

    Answer: [   ]

15. If 3 per cent of the price is £24, how much is the full price?

    A £600   B £240   C £750   D £850   E £400   F £800

    Answer: [   ]

16. A company is running a special promotion and is discounting its product by 25 per cent. If the price before the discount was £10 and the total revenue was £1,000, by what percentage should sales increase to generate the same amount of revenue as before the reduction?

    A 7.5%   B 25%   C 10%   D 33.3%   E 12.5%   F 15%

    Answer: [   ]

17. If a package contains four boxes of staples and each consecutive box is 50 per cent heavier than the previous one, how heavy is the heaviest box if the total weight of the package is 1 kg? Round your answer up to the nearest gram.

    A 500 g   B 300 g   C 450 g   D 685 g   E 416 g   F 725 g

    Answer: [   ]

18. Sales staff A and B are selling the same product. A sold £1,000 worth of products and received 3.5 per cent commission, while B received only 3 per cent. How many more sales should B realize to achieve the same amount of commission as A?

A £50.67   B £96.76   C £166.67   D £186.76

Answer:

19. A videoconference is to take place between Dubai, London and New York. If Dubai is four hours behind London and New York is six hours ahead of London, and if the conference is to start at 2.30 pm on 11 January New York time, what time will it start in Dubai?

A 00.30 am 10 Jan   B 02.30 am 10 Jan   C 00.30 am 11 Jan
D 02.30 am 11 Jan   E 04.30 am 11 Jan   F 02.30 am 12 Jan

Answer:

20. 20 per cent of office workers travel to work by car, 70 per cent by train and 10 per cent by bus. Express these values as a ratio.

A 2:3.5:1   B 1:1.6:2   C 2:2.5:1   D 2:2.5:1.5
E 1.5:2.5:1   F 1:3.5:0.5

Answer:

21. Express 3/20 as a percentage.

A 10%   B 20%   C 13.5%   D 15%   E 22.5%   F 35%

Answer:

22. One metre of optical fibre cable is priced at £7.99. Calculate the price of one foot of cable, if 1 ft = 0.305 m.

A £4.50   B £7.68   C £2.99   D £3.99   E £2.25   F £2.44

Answer:

23. The maximum weight allowed in the office elevator is 225 kg. What is the maximum weight allowed expressed in lbs, if 1 lb = 0.45 kg?

A 499.50 lb   B 500.00 lb   C 101.25 lb   D 370.00 lb
E 350.00 lb   F 325.00 lb

Answer: [   ]

24. If a vehicle travels at 35 mph, how many kilometres would it travel in 30 minutes if 1 km = 0.621 miles?

A 33 km   B 56 km   C 28 km   D 66 km   E 18 km   F 17.5 km

Answer: [   ]

25. Kim usually flies from Heathrow, and her taxi fare to the airport is on average £12 for a 25-minute drive. This time, however, Kim is flying from Luton and the taxi drive will take 45 min. Assuming taxi fares are proportionate to the time taken, how much should Kim expect to pay for her drive to Luton airport?

A £15.60   B £16.20   C £21.60   D £20.60   E £12.60
F £6.20

Answer: [   ]

26. The price of laminated flooring is £6.25 per sq ft. How much would it cost to buy enough flooring to cover 5 sq m if 1 ft = 0.305 m? Calculate the answer to the nearest pound.

A £314   B £150   C £218   D £298   E £336   F £170

Answer: [   ]

27. Frank takes pride in achieving an average of 35 mph during his journey to work of 25 miles. However, in the evening his same journey home takes twice as long. What is Frank's daily average speed?

    A 15.25 mph   B 25.25 mph   C 18.25 mph   D 26.25 mph
    E 30.25 mph   F 20.25 mph

    Answer: [   ]

28. In January a project team spent 50 per cent of its total budget plus £1,000. In February 50 per cent of the remainder was spent plus a further £1,000. If at the start of March the project team still had £5,000 of the budgeted amount at its disposal, how much was the total budget assigned?

    A £25,000   B £26,000   C £16,000   D £17,500
    E £24,000   F £15,000

    Answer: [   ]

29. A shelf in a storage room is 1.83 m wide. How many files can be stored if the width of a single file is 1 inch? (1 inch = 0.083 ft; 1 ft = 0.305 m.)

    A 6   B 12   C 60   D 84   E 70   F 72

    Answer: [   ]

30. Marie leaves her house at 7.30 am and arrives at the office at 9 am. If the distance between Marie's house and the office is 56 miles and if she takes a 20-minute break halfway, what is the average speed Marie should drive to arrive on time?

    A 45 mph   B 48 mph   C 58 mph   D 37.8 mph   E 43 mph
    F 27.5 mph

    Answer: [   ]

End of test.

Practice test 2: data interpretation

This test consists of 24 questions. Allow yourself 20 minutes to complete it.

The tests are made up of a number of tables or graphs of numerical information which are followed by a series of questions relating to each of the tables or graphs. There is a list of suggested answers to each question and it is your task to identify the correct answer. Indicate your answer by writing the letter of the correct answer, A–F, in the answer box.

This style of test is becoming extremely common and will test both your ability to interpret information presented graphically and a wide range of numerical competencies. Expect to be tested in, for example, the operation of percentages, ratios, fractions and averages, and the conversion of units of currency or measurements.

Use a calculator if you need to, but try to use it only sparingly. Use scrap paper to do rough workings. Remember to practice educated guessing.

Stick strictly to the recommended time and try hard to get the best possible score.

Do not turn the page until you are ready to begin.

Data interpretation

Table 3.1   Market research findings on the preferred colour of pre-paid vouchers

Total no. of interviewees	Age group	Positive responses by preferred colour			
		Green	Blue	Pink	Red
200	15–25	58	45	33	64
200	26–35	68	53	40	39
300	36–45	42	93	70	95
160	46–55	48	56	16	40
90	56–65	25	18	30	17
50	66–75	11	15	10	14

1.   Which age group most favoured the green pre-paid vouchers?

A 15–25   B 26–35   C 36–45   D 46–55   E 56–65
F 66–75

Answer: [   ]

2.   How many interviewees most favoured the red vouchers?

A 113   B 325   C 244   D 269   E 332   F 543

Answer: [   ]

3.   What percentage of those aged 15–25 favoured the pink vouchers?

A 12%   B 17.5%   C 22%   D 16.5%   E 66.66%
F 33.33%

Answer: [   ]

4. Which age group was the least favourable to green vouchers in percentage terms?

    A 15–25   B 26–35   C 36–45   D 46–55   E 56–65
    F 66–75

    Answer: [   ]

Table 3.2 shows the current currency exchange rate into pounds sterling. The commission charged per transaction is 4.5 per cent.

Table 3.2   Currency exchange rate into pounds sterling

Country	Currency	Selling price	Buying price	Remarks
Australia	Dollar	2.79	2.99	–
Turkey	Lira	–	24.49	–
South Africa	Rand	3.18	3.38	–
Israel	Shekel	–	591.86	500 and above
New Zealand	Dollar	5.76	6.18	10 and above
Eurozone	Euro	1.55	1.66	–

5. Claire went to South Africa and returned with 280 rands. How much will she get, before commission, if she sells them at the current rate?

    A £82.67   B £75.55   C £79.11   D £82.84   E £88.05
    F £84.08

    Answer: [   ]

6. A company is sending its executives on a business trip to Australia, and the total cash allowance is £1,750. How many Australian dollars can be purchased after paying the commission?

    A 580.78   B 4,997.03   C 5,019.88   D 5,102.21
    E 5,467.96   F 599.01

    Answer: [   ]

7. The trip to Australia (see Question 6) was cancelled at the last minute, so the company decided to change the unneeded Australian dollars back into pounds. How much in £ sterling did it receive, after paying commission?

A £1,750.00   B £1,791.05   C £13,314.00   D £1,596.04
E £1,710.45   F £4,997.03

Answer: [   ]

8. Take the average of the selling and buying price for the euro and use it to calculate 0.5 euro expressed in pounds.

A £0.31   B £0.62   C £0.27   D £0.95   E £0.25   F £0.81

Answer: [   ]

Table 3.3   Bank account holder records

Account holder	Initial balance (£)	Money deposited (£)	Money withdrawn (£)
S. Davies	23.45	0	20.00
H. Gomez	227.50	50.00	270.00
J.K. Josef	386.16	12.50	0
O. McCormack	−250.00	360.00	25.00
F. Wild	−76.50	50.00	0
D. Zair	36.00	6.00	40.00

9. What percentage of account holders are overdrawn?

A 15%   B 33.33%   C 19%   D 16.66%   E 24.5%
F 17.5%

Answer: [   ]

10. If F. Wild deposits £2 every fortnight, makes no more with-drawals and is charged no interest or fees, how many weeks will it take before his overdraft is paid off in full?

A 13.2   B 53   C 6.6   D 12.3   E 25.6   F 26.5

Answer:

11. If S. Davis's salary of £800 is deposited on 4 February and her rent of £95 is debited on the same day, what will her balance be on 5 February?

A £750.00   B £709.45   C £708.45   D £705.00
E £728.50   F £748.00

Answer:

12. What is O. McCormack's final balance?

A £85.00   B £155.00   C £135.00   D £90.00   E £45.00
F £68.00

Answer:

Table 3.4   Postage rates

UK	Weight up to:	60g	100g	150g	200g	300g	400g	500g	Each extra 250g
	First class (£)	0.27	0.41	0.57	0.72	0.96	1.30	1.66	0.85
	Second class (£)	0.19	0.33	0.44	0.54	0.76	1.05	–	–
Worldwide	Weight up to:	10g	20g	40g	60g	80g	100g	Each extra 50g	
	Europe	x	0.37	0.52	0.68	0.84	0.99	0.59	
	W Zone 1	0.47	0.68	1.05	1.42	1.79	2.16	1.25	
	W Zone 2	0.47	0.68	1.12	1.56	2.00	2.44	1.40	

13. A first-class package to Aberdeen weights 550 g and a letter to France weights 12 g. According to Table 3.4, how much is the total postage?

    A £2.03   B £2.55   C £2.88   D £2.50   E £3.00   F £3.88

    Answer: [   ]

14. A first-class package to Dover weights 0.96 kg. How much is the total postage?

    A £3.36   B £2.51   C £3.15   D £2.15   E £2.36   F £3.51

    Answer: [   ]

15. A packet to Europe is three and a half times lighter than a 350 g packet to the UK, posted first-class. How much would it cost to post both packets?

    A £1.95   B £4.30   C £2.12   D £3.50   E £3.29   F £2.29

    Answer: [   ]

16. A first letter to W Zone 1 weighs 40 g, and a second letter to the same destination weighs 65 g. What would the difference in price be if the letters were sent together as a single letter or separately?

    A £1.18   B £1.23   C £0.26   D £0.47   E £0.57   F £0.95

    Answer: [   ]

Table 3.5   Mortality and birth rates, 2001

Country	Population in millions	Births per thousand	Deaths per thousand
Germany	83	9.15	9.2
France	60	12	9
Italy	58	9.05	10.05
Spain	40	9.25	9.15
United Kingdom	60	11.54	10.35
Holland	16	8.69	7.85

17. What was the total number of deaths in Germany during the year?

A 9,200   B 763,600   C 92,000   D 76,300   E 7,630
F 184,000

Answer:

18. What was the total increase in population in France?

A 720,000   B 180,000   C 300,000   D 18,000
E 72,000   F 640,000

Answer:

19. If the population growth per year remained the same, what would the total French population have been at the end of 2002?

A 60,360,000   B 60,000,360   C 60,360,540
D 60,366,000   E 63,600,000   F 63,654,000

Answer:

20. Which countries are experiencing a decrease in population?

A France and England   B England and Germany
C Spain and Italy   D Holland and Spain
E Italy and Germany   F Germany and France

Answer:

Table 3.6   Areas of land, water and arable land, 2006

Country	Total area (sq km)	Land	Water	Arable land, permanent pastures and woodland (%)
Germany	357,021	349,223	7,798	33
France	547,030	545,630	1,400	33
Italy	301,230	294,020	7,210	31
Spain	504,782	499,542	5,240	30
England	244,820	241,590	3,230	25
Holland	41,526	33,883	7,643	25

21. How many sq km of land are there in France if you exclude the arable land, permanent pasture and woodlands?

    A 113,810 sq km   B 192,700 sq km   C 366,510 sq km
    D 180,058 sq km   E 118,410 sq km   F 365,572 sq km

    Answer:

22. What is the total area of Holland expressed in sq miles, if 1 mile = 1.6 km? Round your answer to the nearest sq mile.

    A 19,125 sq m   B 27,750 sq m   C 16,195 sq m
    D 27,075 sq m   E 27,065 sq m   F 18,195 sq m

    Answer:

23. What percentage of Holland's total territory is covered by water?
    A 17%   B 0.17%   C 1.3%   D 12.3%   E 9.5%   F 18.4%

    Answer:

24. What area of total Spanish territory is covered by arable land, permanent pastures and woodland?

A 253,445.00 sq km   B 353,347.50 sq km
C 355,723.50 sq km   D 188,670.00 sq km
E 199,887.00 sq km   F 151,434.50 sq km

Answer: [   ]

End of test.

Practice test 3: correct sentences

This test comprises 20 questions. Allow yourself eight minutes to complete it.

Each question comprises a number of versions of the same sentence, only one of which is correct in terms of English usage. Your task is to identify the correct sentence. Indicate your answer by writing the letter of the correct answer, a)–d), in the answer box.

Stick strictly to the recommended time limit. Try to manage your time so that you finish all the questions and work as fast as you can until you have answered all the questions or run out of time.

Do not turn the page until you are ready to begin.

Correct sentences

1. a) If she's only listened to me, this would never have happened.
    b) If she had only listened to me, this would never have happened.
    c) If she will only listen to me, this will never have happend.
    d) None of these.

    Answer: [   ]

2. a) There's just three thing's you need to know about Jack.
    b) There's just three things you need to know about Jack.
    c) There are just three things you need to know about Jack.
    d) None of these.

    Answer: [   ]

3. a) If I was you I've seen a doctor.
    b) If I were you I'd see a doctor.
    c) If I was you I'll see a doctor.
    d) None of these.

    Answer: [   ]

4. a) It looks like everyone has gone to the cinema.
    b) It looked like everyone has gone to the cinema.
    c) It looks like everyone had gone to the cinema.
    d) None of these.

    Answer: [   ]

5. a) Either Jane or her sister are bringing the dessert.
    b) Either Jane or her sister is bringing the dessert.
    c) Either Jane or her sister were bringing the dessert.
    d) None of these.

    Answer: [   ]

6. a) If I hadn't had my seatbelt on I'll be dead.
    b) If I didn't have my seatbelt on I'll have been dead.
    c) If I hadn't had my seatbelt on I would be dead.
    d) None of these.

    Answer: [   ]

7. a) From Thursday you cannot have either the blue nor the black pens.
    b) From Thursday you cannot have either the blue or the black pens.
    c) From Thursday you cannot have neither the blue nor the black pens.
    d) None of these.

    Answer: [   ]

8. a) I have been informed that neither Mandy nor Helen will be able to be there on Saturday.
    b) I have been informed that neither Mandy or Helen will be able to be there on Saturday.
    c) I have been informed that not either Mandy or Helen will be able to be there on Saturday.
    d) None of these.

    Answer: [   ]

9. a) Owning a dog is very different to owning a cat.
    b) Owning a dog is very different from owning a cat.
    c) Owning a dog is very different over owning a cat.
    d) None of these.

    Answer: [   ]

10. a) Compared with analogue TV, digital TV provided the consumer with a greater choice of programmes to watch.
    b) Compared to analogue TV, digital TV providing the consumer with a greater choice of programmes to watch.
    c) Compared to analogue TV, digital TV provided the consumer with a greater choice of programmes to watch.
    d) None of these.

Answer: [   ]

11. a) If you was to go fishing at night you will find that you caught more fish than during the day.
    b) If you was to go fishing at night you might find that you catch more fish than during the day.
    c) If you were to go fishing at night you might find that you caught more fish than during the day.
    d) None of these.

Answer: [   ]

12. a) Although the house and barn are on the same property, they will be sold separately.
    b) Although the house and barn were on the same property, they will be sold separately.
    c) Although the house and barn was on the same property, they were to be sold separately.
    d) None of these.

Answer: [   ]

13. a) The school have insisted that no child leaves the playground until their parent arrive.
    b) The school has insisted that no children leaves the playground until their parent arrives.
    c) The school have insisted that no child leaves the playground until their parent arrived.
    d) None of these.

Answer: [   ]

14. a) The Managing Director wanted you and I to attend the
         meeting.
     b) The Managing Director wanted you and me to attend the
         meeting.
     c) The Managing Director wanted me and you to attend the
         meeting.
     d) None of these.

Answer:

15. a) Each night before I go to bed I made myself a cup of cocoa.
     b) Each night before I go to bed I make myself a cup of cocoa.
     c) Each night before I go to bed I makes myself a cup of cocoa.
     d) None of these.

Answer:

16. a) Carol thought it an honour to receive an MBE.
     b) Carol thought it a honour to receive an MBE.
     c) Carol thought it an honour to receive a MBE.
     d) None of these.

Answer:

17. a) It looks like it's going to rain.
     b) It looks like it's about to rain.
     c) It looks as if it is going to rain.
     d) None of these.

Answer:

18. a) Every one of the new computers in the main office have been virus checked.
    b) Every one of the new computers in the main office has been virus checked.
    c) Every one of the new computers in the main office been virus checked.
    d) None of these.

    Answer: [   ]

19. a) It is equally important to check your credit card statement as it is your bank statement.
    b) It is equally as important to cheque your credit card statement as it is your bank statement.
    c) It is equally as important to check your credit card statement as it is your bank statement.
    d) None of these.

    Answer: [   ]

20. a) Mike seems to always do it that way.
    b) Mike seems to do it that way always.
    c) Mike always seems to do it that way.
    d) None of these.

    Answer: [   ]

End of test.

Practice test 4: following procedures

There are 17 questions to be completed in 12 minutes.

In this test you are provided with some information, such as an organizational chart or description of a hypothetical situation, and some rules that apply to how you should proceed. Below each set of information and rules is a series of questions that you must answer by referring to the information and rules. Each question includes a list of suggested answers. Note that for some questions more than one suggested answer may be correct. Indicate your answer by writing the letter(s) of the correct answer(s) in the answer box.

Keep to the recommended time limit.

Do not turn the page until you are ready to begin.

Following procedures

Situation 1

Figure 3.1   Organizational chart

List of approved suppliers

Wittlys Plc
Echomax UK
Dublin Bay Supplies
Docklands Electrical
Global Solutions Inc.

Rules governing purchases in a procurement department

Staff may approve any purchase subject to the following limitations:

- All purchases over £100,000 must be approved by the appropriate area manager and by Mr D. Fryer.
- All purchases from a supplier not on the approved-supplier list can only be approved by the regional manager.
- Area managers may approve expenditure in their area and from approved suppliers up to a value of £100,000, or for other areas from approved suppliers up to a value of £70,000.
- Within their area, and only with approved suppliers, executive officers may approve purchases to a maximum of £5,000, and administrative officers may approve of purchases to a maximum of £1,000,
- Administrative assistants may not approve purchases over £199.
- Susan Dale may approve expenditure to a value of £70,000.

1. Name the member(s) of staff who can approve a purchase for £200 from Island Consultants.

    A Susan Dale   B Susan Hays   C Andy Jones   D Fay Kemp
    E Mr D. Fryer   F Rita French

    Answer:

2. Which officer or manager (not director) can approve a purchase of £80,000 for Area 2 from Global Solutions Inc?

    A Rita French   B Tom Mosby   C Maria Key   D Susan Hays
    E Paul Sheen   F Diana Jordan   G Alex Matthews
    H Andy Jones

    Answer: [   ]

3. Which administrative officer(s) can approve a purchase from Wittlys PLC for Area 1 to the value of £1,000?

    A Diana Jordan   B Alex Matthews   C Andy Jones   D None

    Answer: [   ]

4. Which of the following may not approve a purchase of £70,000 for Area 1 from Echomax UK?

    A Regional Director   B Susan Dale   C Rita French
    D Tom Mosby   E Maria Key

    Answer: [   ]

5. How many of the following staff are required to approve a purchase of over £100,000 from Dockland Electrical for Area 2?

    Mr D. Fryer, Susan Dale, Rita French, Tom Mosby, Maria Key, Susan Hays, Paul Sheen

    A 1   B 2   C 3   D 4   E 5   F 6   G 7

    Answer: [   ]

Situation 2

Robin commissioned an employment agency to fill a position in his company. The agency's fees are based on a percentage of the first year's remuneration. The agencies terms allow for them to add tax to the total due at 15 per cent.

The terms of business of the agency stated that:

- Fixed-term contracts are charged at an apportioned pro-rata basis of permanent fees.
- If the introduced employee leaves within eight weeks of starting employment, a 100 per cent rebate applies. If the employee leaves after eight weeks and before 12 weeks, a 50 per cent rebate applies; if the employee leaves after 12 weeks but before 20 weeks, a 25 per cent rebate is given.
- If the remuneration includes the provision of a car, the sum of £2,000 shall be added to the first year's remuneration for purposes of calculating the introduction fee (irrespective of whether the contract is permanent or fixed term).
- For annual remuneration up to £15,999, the introduction fee is 16 per cent; between £16,000 and £19,999, it is 20 per cent; and over £20,000 it is 25 per cent.

---

6. What percentage would be used to calculate the introduction fee if the position to be filled was permanent, and paid £20,000 a year with no other benefits?

    A 16%   B 20%   C 25%   D Insufficient information to tell

    Answer: _____

7. If after 10 weeks of employment the introduced employee left the company's employment, what kind of rebate should Robin expect on the bill?

A 100%   B 50%   C 25%   D None

Answer:

8   What fee should Robin expect if the employee was to start on a fixed-term contract of employment for a term of six months on a salary of £16,000 per annum plus the benefit of a car?

A   Insufficient information to answer
B   20% of £16,000 ÷ 2 (apportioned pro-rata reduction for six months fixed term)
C   25% of 18,000 ÷ 2 (apportioned pro-rata reduction for six months fixed term)
D   20% of 18,000 ÷ 2 (apportioned pro-rata reduction for six months fixed term)
E   25% of £9,000 plus 15% tax
F   20% of £,10,000 plus 15% tax

Answer:

Situation 3

Mrs Smith is the manager of the accounts-due department in a busy builders' merchants. She has an assistant, Tina, and between them they are responsible for issuing 10,000 invoices a year and collecting payments against them. Mrs Smith's line manager is Mr Jones the company accountant, with whom she meets weekly. At this meeting they review all accounts on which an invoice is overdue and all disputed invoices, and decide whether or not to refer an account to the company's firm of solicitors for advice as to whether there is a case for issuing legal proceedings. (Mrs Smith is responsible for carrying out all the decisions made at this meeting except the issuing of legal proceedings, which is done by a firm of solicitors.)

It is the responsibility of sales staff to ensure that all customers agree to the company's terms of business before the company will accept an order. Sales staff may not accept further orders from customers whose accounts have any overdue invoices against them.

Mrs Smith and her assistant operate according to the following procedures:

- The company's terms of business state that payment must be received within 15 working days of the receipt of goods and that notice of faulty or incomplete goods must be given within 5 working days.
- Invoices are issued on the same day as the good are dispatched, the first reminder is sent out after 5 working days and the final reminder on the 15th working day notifying the customer that the invoice is overdue and that payment must be made immediately.

9. What action(s) should Mrs Smith take if a new customer has failed to pay an invoice within 15 working days of receipt of the goods?

   A Refer the customer to the appointed firm of solicitors.
   B Confirm with sales staff that the customer did indeed agree to the terms of business before the order was accepted.
   C Issue a reminder.
   D Refuse any further orders from that customer.
   E Resolve to review the account with Mr Jones at their next meeting.

   Answer: [   ]

10 Whose responsibility is it to collect payments against the 10,000 invoices issued each year?

   A Mr Jones   B Mrs Smith   C The sales staff   D Tina
   E It is not possible to say

   Answer: [   ]

11   Mr Jones and Mrs Smith decide whether or not to:

    A   Issue legal proceedings against disputed invoices.
    B   Issue legal proceedings against overdue invoices.
    C   Issue legal proceedings against both disputed and overdue invoices.
    D   None of these.

Answer: [   ]

Situation 4

An applicant to an industrial tribunal complained that she had been the victim of sexual discrimination on the grounds that she had received a lower percentage salary increase than some of her male colleagues. In deciding the case the tribunal referred to the following rules. Use them to answer the questions that follow.

Rules

1.   It is for the applicant to make out his or her case on the balance of probabilities.
2.   It is unusual to find direct evidence of sexual discrimination, and few employers will be prepared to admit such discrimination.
3.   The outcome of a case depends on what inferences it is proper to draw from the primary facts found by the tribunal.
4.   A finding of discrimination and a finding of a difference in gender will often point to the possibility of sexual discrimination. In such circumstances the tribunal will look to the employer for an explanation.
5.   At the conclusions of all the evidence the tribunal should reach a conclusion, bearing in mind the difficulties which face a person who complains of unlawful discrimination and the fact that it is for the complainant to prove his or her case.

---

12. Which of the following pieces of information would least support the applicant's case?

   A   The applicant was unable to present evidence of direct discrimination on the ground of gender.
   B   The employer denied discrimination on the ground of gender.
   C   The tribunal concluded that the applicant was unable to prove her case on the balance of probability.
   D   The employer admitted indirectly discriminating on the basis of gender.

   Answer:

13. What would you expect the tribunal to do if the applicant demonstrated on the balance of probability that she had been treated differently?

   A   Ask the employer to explain the unequal treatment.
   B   Conclude the employer had discriminated unfairly.
   C   Award an unlimited sum in compensation.
   D   Conclude that direct discrimination on the ground of gender had taken place.
   E   None of these.

   Answer:

14. Which piece of information would best explain the tribunal's conclusion that the applicant's claim had failed?

   A   Evidence presented showed that she had received a 3 per cent increase, in line with most other employees.
   B   The employer provided explanations to demonstrate that the exceptions were all for good reason.
   C   Mr Smith had had a higher percentage increase to bring him up to the same salary as the applicant, and had been paid too little before that pay rise.
   D   Mr Gamble had received no pay rise at all because his recent review had found him to be ineffective in his post.

   Answer:

Situation 5

A stakeholder pension is a tax-efficient way of saving specifically for retirement. Savers are provided with their own plan and are sent regular statements showing the value of their fund. Use the stated rules to answer the questions that follow.

Rules

1. All contributions to a stakeholder's pension plan qualify for tax relief at the highest rate paid by the saver, and growth is free of UK income tax and capital gains tax. Fund values are calculated daily.
2. Management charges are due and calculated each day on the basis of the value of the fund on that day. The fee is based on 1/365th of the appropriate rate of the annual management fee.
3. Providers charge according to a tiered series of charges, with qualifying levels dependent on the saver's fund value.
   - For funds valued at up to £15,000 the fee is 1.25 per cent.
   - For funds valued between £15,000 and £25,000 the fee is 1 per cent.
   - For funds valued between £25,000 and £50,000 the fee is 0.8 per cent.
   - For funds valued at over £50,000 the fee is 0.6 per cent.

---

15. What level of management charge will a stakeholder pension provider make against a saver with a fund valued at £50,000?

    A 1.25%   B 1%   C 0.8%   D 0.6%

    Answer: [   ]

16. Stakeholder pension providers are not allowed to charge more than a maximum annual management fee of 1.25 per cent of the fund value.

    A True   B False   C Cannot tell

    Answer:

17. A saver complains that he has been overcharged as a management fee of 1/365th of 1 per cent per day was applied to his fund with a value of £14,000; is he right in his assertion?

    A. Yes, he has been overcharged.
    B. No, he has not been overcharged.
    C. The calculation is correct.
    D. It is not possible to tell.

    Answer:

End of test

Practice test 5: speed and accuracy

This test has 50 questions to be attempted in six minutes.

Each question comprises four pairs of numbers and letters arranged in two columns. It is your task to identify how many pairs of numbers and letters are identical in both columns. You are offered five possible answers: one pair, two pairs, three pairs, four pairs or none. Indicate your answer by writing the letter of the correct answer, A–E, in the answer box.

This is obviously a test of working fast and accurately.

With practice you can greatly improve your speed in this type of test.

Keep strictly to the suggested time limit and stop when the time is up.

Do not turn the page until you are ready to begin.

Speed and accuracy

1. YRCK2971   YRCK2971
    9020PXZ3   9020PXZ3
    ALGY8431   ALGV8431
    467111PQK   46711PQK
    A 1 pair B 2 pairs C 3 pairs D 4 pairs E none

    Answer:

2. 0000412P   0000412P
    12123DF   12113DF
    XXYG772   XXYG772
    LLXII110   LLXII110
    A 1 pair B 2 pairs C 3 pairs D 4 pairs E none

    Answer:

3. UIUA297   UIUA297
    0021ZPW   0021ZPW
    BJUH211   BJUH121
    99741ILS   99741ILS
    A 1 pair B 2 pairs C 3 pairs D 4 pairs E none

    Answer:

4. LSAT44211   LSAT42211
    1911CCRE   1191CCRE
    AAA00031   AAAA0031
    VTRE7421   VTER7421
    A 1 pair B 2 pairs C 3 pairs D 4 pairs E none

    Answer:

5.   LLL6770   LLL6110
     AKAKI21   AKAKL12
     00003321   00003221
     XXREWQ   XXREWQ
     A 1 pair   B 2 pairs   C 3 pairs   D 4 pairs   E none

     Answer:

6.   999321SS   999321SS
     01023WQK   01023WQK
     876345CF   876345CF
     1111874RE   1111874RE
     A 1 pair   B 2 pairs   C 3 pairs   D 4 pairs   E none

     Answer:

7.   975985AS   975985AS
     AS975985   AS975985
     97AS5958   97AS5958
     AS599785   AS975985
     A 1 pair   B 2 pairs   C 3 pairs   D 4 pairs   E none

     Answer:

8.   50515052Q   50515052Q
     456789CCF   457689CCF
     XOIU1113   XOUI1113
     AAAKI334   AAKII334
     A 1 pair   B 2 pairs   C 3 pairs   D 4 pairs   E none

     Answer:

9. QQWE4456   QQWU4456
    754BBRT1   754BBTR1
    8UWQ321   8UQW321
    BEWQ908   BEWO908
    A 1 pair B 2 pairs C 3 pairs D 4 pairs E none

    Answer:

10. VVVTT332   VVVT3332
    CCCV8871   CCCW8871
    33541FFDE   333451FFDE
    4498XXEW   4988XXEW
    A 1 pair B 2 pairs C 3 pairs D 4 pairs E none

    Answer:

11. 11221ZZW   11221ZZW
    ZZWW1122   ZZWW1122
    11ZZWW22   11ZWWW22
    222ZZWW1   222ZZWW1
    A 1 pair B 2 pairs C 3 pairs D 4 pairs E none

    Answer:

12. XDMK2220   XDMK2200
    NNNJU454   NNNJU545
    ZWPLO081   ZWPLO811
    NNJU2121   NNJU1212
    A 1 pair B 2 pairs C 3 pairs D 4 pairs E none

    Answer:

13. LLKII2245   LLKII2445
     2445KIILL   2245KIILL
     LKL11245   LKL12145
     12145LKL   12145LKL
     A 1 pair   B 2 pairs   C 3 pairs   D 4 pairs   E none

     Answer: [   ]

14. OOOO332   OOO3332
     33220000Q   3322000Q
     O332Q000   O332Q000
     OOOQ233   OOOQ233
     A 1 pair   B 2 pairs   C 3 pairs   D 4 pairs   E none

     Answer: [   ]

15. LOLL2231   LOL22231
     77208XKX   77280XKX
     AW34KI81   AW34KI81
     CC873KIQ   CC837KIQ
     A 1 pair   B 2 pairs   C 3 pairs   D 4 pairs   E none

     Answer: [   ]

16. HUHI5467   HUHI5467
     QPAL2881   QPAL2881
     2313XRV1   2313XRV1
     99921VTR   99921VTR
     A 1 pair   B 2 pairs   C 3 pairs   D 4 pairs   E none

     Answer: [   ]

17. 000112XD   001112XD
    XD110002   XD11002
    CRRC343   CRRC343
    2323VVG   2323VVG
    A 1 pair   B 2 pairs   C 3 pairs   D 4 pairs   E none

    Answer: [   ]

18. 874301VWV   873401VWV
    ZZZ220011   ZZ2220011
    2220011XX   222011XX
    LPPIO9111   LPPIO9111
    A 1 pair   B 2 pairs   C 3 pairs   D 4 pairs   E none

    Answer: [   ]

19. 00873BBHU   00878BBHU
    BBUH00738   BPUH00738
    BPUH78700   BPUH87800
    BBHU78700   BPUH78700
    A 1 pair   B 2 pairs   C 3 pairs   D 4 pairs   E none

    Answer: [   ]

20. 984560XXY   985460XXY
    77442CCG1   77442CCG1
    00101X0X1   00101X0X1
    020274V0V   020274V0V
    A 1 pair   B 2 pairs   C 3 pairs   D 4 pairs   E none

    Answer: [   ]

21.   00000333   0000333
      3333000   33330000
      1110001   11100001
      1000001   10000001
      A 1 pair   B 2 pairs   C 3 pairs   D 4 pairs   E none

      Answer: [   ]

22.   HH2349EW   HH2349EW
      VV8815829   VV8814829
      18357AEM   18857AEM
      AEMM3921   AEM3921
      A 1 pair   B 2 pairs   C 3 pairs   D 4 pairs   E none

      Answer: [   ]

23.   SS32109UI   SS32109UI
      459821XFL   459821XFL
      NUEE90123   NUEE90123
      CUQOS321   CUQOS321
      A 1 pair   B 2 pairs   C 3 pairs   D 4 pairs   E none

      Answer: [   ]

24.   QOOQW187   QOQOW187
      IVVII23910   IVIIV23910
      UCV.29870   UCV.29870
      XHQ/4002   XHQ\4002
      A 1 pair   B 2 pairs   C 3 pairs   D 4 pairs   E none

      Answer: [   ]

25. 10000011   10000011
    33300000   33300000
    66000006   66000006
    99999911   99999911
    A 1 pair B 2 pairs C 3 pairs D 4 pairs E none

    Answer: [   ]

26. PO89XV22   PO89XV22
    LPCDDVDM3   LPCDDVDMP3
    999101EMG   99101EMG
    10.901.87   10.0109.87
    A 1 pair B 2 pairs C 3 pairs D 4 pairs E none

    Answer: [   ]

27. 10.901.87   10.901.87
    10.901.88   10.901.88
    10.901.89   10.901.90
    10.901.90   10.901.91
    A 1 pair B 2 pairs C 3 pairs D 4 pairs E none

    Answer: [   ]

28. WA427319A   WA427139A
    QS982309B   QS892309B
    CV459889A   CV459889A
    ZX923405B   XZ923405B
    A 1 pair B 2 pairs C 3 pairs D 4 pairs E none

    Answer: [   ]

29. \0910PE33D   0910PE33D
     D880PE106/   D880PE106\
     \091D8833P   \91D8333P
     D01YE107/   D10YE107/
     A 1 pair   B 2 pairs   C 3 pairs   D 4 pairs   E none

     Answer: [   ]

30. AAAAIIII   AAAAIIII
     IIIIIAAAA   IIIIIAAAA
     AIAIAIAI   AIAIAIA
     AAAIIIAA   AAAIIAA
     A 1 pair   B 2 pairs   C 3 pairs   D 4 pairs   E none

     Answer: [   ]

31. 5LN5COL17   5LN5COL17
     13 15111 04   13 1551 04
     27 1862 07   27 1826 07
     787 2935 72   787 2935 72
     A 1 pair   B 2 pairs   C 3 pairs   D 4 pairs   E none

     Answer: [   ]

32. KMK16–Q001   KMK16–Q001
     KMK-BBOB1   KMK-BBOB1
     KMMME352   KMMME352
     KMK14–N010PC   KMK14–N010PC
     A 1 pair   B 2 pairs   C 3 pairs   D 4 pairs   E none

     Answer: [   ]

33. KMPB50024V   KMBP50012V
    LED5MM12V   LED4MM12V
    DJZI24140A   DJZI24140A
    VSDRPCSV   VSDRPCSV
    A 1 pair   B 2 pairs   C 3 pairs   D 4 pairs   E none

Answer:

34. K6.5 EFOZ   K6.5EFOZ
    K27EFOZSS   K27EFOZSS
    DJZL24140A   DJZL24120A
    EPOS24VDC   EPOS240VDC
    A 1 pair   B 2 pairs   C 3 pairs   D 4 pairs   E none

Answer:

35. 800000011   80000011
    62222299   62222999
    77771110   77771110
    55555999   55555999
    A 1 pair   B 2 pairs   C 3 pairs   D 4 pairs   E none

Answer:

36. A00RGS3B11   A00RGSB311
    Q01SP1B16   Q01PS1B16
    24V2X100   24V2X100
    100W24VSP33   10W24VSP33
    A 1 pair   B 2 pairs   C 3 pairs   D 4 pairs   E none

Answer:

37. MEAMM30/2   MEAMM32/0
     MEAMM32/0   MEAMM30/2
     AQUAIR100   AQUAIRR100
     SRPV7D12   SRPV7D12
     A 1 pair   B 2 pairs   C 3 pairs   D 4 pairs   E none

     Answer:

38. SRCMLPV7D   SRCMLPV7D
     SPUS116FC   SPUS116FC
     W01SPA00RG   W01SPA00RG
     A00RGDB19   A00RGDB19
     A 1 pair   B 2 pairs   C 3 pairs   D 4 pairs   E none

     Answer:

39. INV32008   INV320008
     INV320008   INV32008
     INV3756   INV3576
     INV8532   INV8523
     A 1 pair   B 2 pairs   C 3 pairs   D 4 pairs   E none

     Answer:

40. 77777222   777777222
     00000004   00000044
     1000004   10000004
     5666633   5666333
     A 1 pair   B 2 pairs   C 3 pairs   D 4 pairs   E none

     Answer:

41. 3981CH10.20   3981CH10.20
     3944a22.58   3944a22.58
     NR210020mm   NR210020mm
     NR207MOKKEN   NR207MOKKERK
     A 1 pair B 2 pairs C 3 pairs   D 4 pairs   E none

     Answer: [   ]

42. BY313634X6X6.5   BY313643X6X6.5
     BY29521.5X9X9.5   BY29512.5X9X9.5
     BY21.5X9X7   BY21.5X9X7
     BY38.6X9X4.3   BY38.6X9X4.3
     A 1 pair B 2 pairs C 3 pairs   D 4 pairs   E none

     Answer: [   ]

43. 303579x65x7F   303579x65x7F
     204360x16x1.8   204360x16x1.8
     3057 San Remo   3057 San Remo
     3057 Mallorca   3057 Mallorca
     A 1 pair B 2 pairs C 3 pairs   D 4 pairs   E none

     Answer: [   ]

44. SGT031LICTHGEN   SGT031LICTHGEN
     SGTO31VERWEND   SGTO31VERWEND
     SIE VERWENDEN   SIE VERWENDEN
     TOO40PORTILEN   TOO40PORTILEN
     A 1 pair B 2 pairs C 3 pairs   D 4 pairs   E none

     Answer: [   ]

45. | | |
    |---|---|
    | 0000000555 | 000000555 |
    | 555555000 | 5555555000 |
    | 050505050 | 05050505050 |
    | 50505050 | 50505050505 |

    A 1 pair   B 2 pairs   C 3 pairs   D 4 pairs   E none

    Answer:

46. | | |
    |---|---|
    | WDKX10PVC | WCKX10PVC |
    | WDKXO9RB | WDKXO9PVC |
    | WDKXO8PVC | WDKXO9PVC |
    | WDKXO7RB | WKDXO7RB |

    A 1 pair   B 2 pairs   C 3 pairs   D 4 pairs   E none

    Answer:

47. | | |
    |---|---|
    | 68969657 | 68969 657 |
    | 68969660 | 68969657 |
    | 68969 | 662 68969662 |
    | 68969 658 | 68969 658 |

    A 1 pair   B 2 pairs   C 3 pairs   D 4 pairs   E none

    Answer:

48. | | |
    |---|---|
    | 205x100x16 | 205x100x16 |
    | 380x85x75 | 38x850x75 |
    | 500x250x150 | 500x250x150 |
    | 240x68x125 | 240x68x125 |

    A 1 pair   B 2 pairs   C 3 pairs   D 4 pairs   E none

    Answer:

49. LH201WHG4   LH201WHG4
     LH160BRUHAN   LH160GRNHAN
     LH92GRNHAN   LH92BRUHAN
     LH140BLUHAN   LH140BLUHAN
     A 1 pair   B 2 pairs   C 3 pairs   D 4 pairs   E none

     Answer:

50. 00000001   0000001
     1111110   11111110
     11100001   11100011
     00001110   00011100
     A 1 pair   B 2 pairs   C 3 pairs   D 4 pairs   E none

     Answer:

End of test

Practice for the Fast Stream

It should be obvious, but let me make it absolutely clear: you will not find everything you need to pass the Fast Stream in this or any other single volume. Success, for many, only follows what amounts to a major commitment. Candidates who pass prepare for each challenge of the application process. They commit many hours to, for example, revising their maths, developing their written style, practising group discussions and improving their interview skills. Very able candidates may fail a stage of the process and yet find the exceptional strength of character to learn from the experience and apply again in the next round. Many succeed only on their third or later attempt.

Over 100 tips and insights into the Fast Stream

There are no hard and fast, sure-fire winning bets when it comes to psychometric tests, and these tips and insights are intended more as food for thought than dos or don'ts. They are intended to inform and raise awareness of key considerations. Use them to tailor your approach to the Fast Stream competition.

General points

- There are many (at least eight) Fast Stream options including the Graduate Fast Stream, GCHQ Cheltenham, Economists, Statisticians, Technology in Business and Clerks in both Houses of Parliament. This list is not exhaustive.
- You need a minimum of a 2:2 degree to apply and must be a British national (see the Fast Stream website for definitions). Some of the specialist Fast Stream options require a 2:1 degree or above.
- If it's not too late to decide which degree to take in order to maximize your chances of success then the overall rate of success by degree type suggests your best chances are if you read economics, a mathematical science, a physical science or engineering (source: inferred from the *Fast Stream Report 2005*).
- Generally the examiners are looking at your writing skills, communications skills, numerical skills, interpersonal and analytical skills and decision-making abilities (source: fast-stream.gov.uk).
- The pass mark is no longer a cut-off – where a certain number of top-scoring candidates are accepted depending on the number of places. Instead a fixed pass mark is likely to be adopted and everyone who achieves it will be offered a place. If many people succeed then you may have a longer wait before being offered a place.

- At certain points in the process you have to use the very basic calculator that is provided. This has very few features (it does have a squared function) so, for example, all other powers have to be calculated in longhand (eg $1.06 \times 1.06 \times 1.06 \times 1.06 \times 1.06$).

- Your age will not count against you as long as you have several years to go before normal retirement age; in fact it may count in your favour as your work experience could greatly help you meet the challenge of the selection process and the role.

- The 'fast' in the Fast Stream is all about the speed of progress through the Civil Service grades. The starting salary may not be great but it does go up considerably as you progress through the grades.

- Some people come out of the exercise feeling sceptical about the value of the whole process. They complain, for example, that the distinction between many of the suggested answers in the qualifying tests and e-tray exercise are so fine that it is as much a case of luck as judgement that you choose the 'right' answer. The tests do involve drawing fine distinctions, many of which are a question of precise judgement, and it takes a great deal of practice to tune in to the examiners' way of thinking.

- Overall just under 4 per cent of applicants are recommended for appointment across all Fast Stream schemes (source: the *Fast Stream Report 2005*).

- The significant 'sift stages' for the graduate Fast Stream are the online tests, e-tray and assessment centre (the recruitment process to schemes for specialists such as economists and statisticians may not have all these stages).

- The first part of the application process is online and consists of a self-assessment, application and battery of online tests. Take great care over your presentation and remember many organizations will reject applications with typos out of hand, so go to the trouble of ensuring that your application is without error. When providing details of your past, check that the dates are correct for both month and year. Ensure addresses, names and titles are complete and 100 per cent accurate. Do not rely on your memory but, for example, go and get the certificates and copy the exact wording, grades and dates.

● You have to register online to begin your application, and will receive a password to access your personal timetable and inbox detailing the stage of your application, details of when you need to have completed stages of the process, invitations to attend events and, perhaps most importantly, results. At faststream.gov.uk they ask that you check both your timetable and inbox regularly.

● Once you are through the first stage of the process your qualifications count for very little. What matters is only how well you do in the various stages of the recruitment process.

The qualifying tests

● In the numerical paper, expect a series of questions that follow economic or social numerical data presented as either tables, pie charts or bar charts. In the verbal paper expect a series of passages followed by questions.

● If the last time you revised your mental arithmetic was when you were preparing for your GCSEs, then do not be at all surprised if you do badly.

● In the numerical paper you do get to use a calculator. Even so, if you take the test when your mental arithmetic is not really sharp then you will probably fail.

● You will find free practice online tests at, for example, www.shl.com and www.psl.co.uk. A word of caution however: many people complain that the Fast Stream questions are much harder than the material found on these sites. Still, they may help to get you started (you have to register).

● All parts of the service use the online tests, although there will be different pass marks for the various Fast Stream options.

● The tests have been simplified considerably since the last edition of this book and now rely on only two question types: data interpretation and verbal reasoning.

- The online tests have largely remained the same for the last two years (at the time of going to print).
- The online practice tests mentioned above are very much like the actual tests (though obviously the questions are different), though they have slightly fewer questions than the real ones.
- To make the most of your preparation, first use the questions in this volume, decide which type represents the greatest challenge and then undertake more extensive practice if necessary. Then, when you are ready, take the online practice tests and real tests.

The numerical tests
- The numerical test is approximately 25 minutes long and comprises around 20 questions.
- You are presented with tables, graphs or charts and asked four questions about each. Expect therefore five charts/graphs for 20 questions.
- Candidates with good mathematical skills say they find the numerical test straightforward and complete it in the time allowed.

The verbal tests
- The verbal test comprises around 40 questions to be completed in about 20 minutes.
- You are presented with a series of paragraphs and have to answer five questions about each. The subjects of the individual paragraphs are often slanted towards business but other subjects are also covered.
- The questions are first and foremost about making judgements.
- It can be extremely difficult to identify the right answers from the list of possible options. As mentioned earlier, there are often very fine distinctions to be made. Some candidates find this irritating and hard to accept when compared with the certainty of the numerical test but you just have to practise to bring your judgement in line with that of the question setters.

- High-scoring candidates complete the tests on time and with a couple of minutes spare to go back and recheck.
- Candidates who have obtained high scores have adopted the following approach: read the passage twice and then reread the relevant bit for each question.

E-tray

'Thanks very much for your advice about the e-tray – it was definitely a critical factor in my success.' (Reader review)

- If you pass the online qualifying tests then you are invited to attend the e-tray exercise.
- Take this next stage in the process very seriously as a large number of candidates fail it.
- You may not have come across anything quite like it before, so take time before attempting the exercise to get familiar with the challenge and to develop your approach.
- The practice e-tray exercise on www.faststream.gov.uk/ does not provide answers, so it is quite hard to know if you are approaching the task correctly. You can find other practice e-tray exercises at: Proposalmaster.co.uk. Try also www.customs.ustreas.gov/xp/cgov/careers/studyguides/ (the proposalmaster exercise was based on this).

The Fast Stream e-tray is split into three parts – Part 1 of the exercise

- In the first part you must read background material. This is likely to include financial information, press articles, academic studies and personnel details of colleagues.
- It is provided onscreen.
- Many people find the time allowed to read all the background material extremely tight.

- Many people come unstuck in Part 1 because they try to take detailed notes. They either find they do not cover all the material, or rush and then cannot decipher their notes later.
- Because of the tight time constraints, rather than trying to take extensive notes you should try indexing the documents so that you can refer back to them when answering questions.

Part 2 of the e-tray exercise

- In the second stage you face an 'inbox' containing 'e-mails', some with attachments.
- Each e-mail is in effect a test question.
- Once you answer one you move on to the next, but cannot return to your previous answer.
- As you progress through the e-mails more arrive.
- This second set of e-mails may be computer adaptive; in other words, their content depends on the answer you gave to the first e-mail.
- The e-mails will relate to a host of issues, including for example points of administration, planning or budgeting, and responses to external bodies, other departments and members of the general public.
- You can and should refer to the background papers to decide your response.
- The e-mails may contain attachments that you should read.
- Because you cannot go back to your previously answered e-mails, time management is critical.
- If you get your timing wrong you may, for example, rush through the e-mails and then find yourself sitting with time to spare having finished the exercise. This is almost bound to mean that you have not spent sufficient time on checking the detail of your answers.
- Some candidates find Stage 2 of the e-tray exercise to be less time pressured than Stage 1.
- In the real exercise, when e-mails start to arrive, you need to refer to the background papers and any attachments to e-mails to decide on your response.

- When selecting appropriate responses take care not to overstep your authority by, for example, entering into binding or implied commitments.
- Different questions will test various capacities. These include: how well you can find your way through the background papers, how good you are at prioritizing, how well you can infer from and apply the information to new situations.
- Make sure you demonstrate the sort of qualities that would make a fantastic Fast Stream candidate: for example balance, integrity, diligence, diplomacy.
- Be especially diplomatic in your handling of the press, outside agencies and other departments.
- Practise writing executive summaries. Do this by abridging articles to two paragraphs or full reports down to two pages.
- It may well help to practise plenty of reading comprehension exercises and critical reasoning tests. Also visit government departments' websites and read as many papers and reports as possible.
- The importance of factual accuracy and attention to detail cannot be overstated. Make sure you get the facts right by referring back. Consider checking figures you are given rather than assuming they are right.
- Success really is in the detail, and seemingly minor points can determine the correct answer. So as you read the briefing documents, look out for and recall what might otherwise be innocent, unimportant points of detail. They can really make all the difference when it comes to the 'e-mails' questions.
- In 2006 a bar at the top of the inbox was added telling you how many e-mails you had answered/ read and how many were in your inbox. Some candidates describe this as making things considerably easier.

Part 3 of the e-tray exercise
- The third stage of the exercise involves your writing a memo.
- The memo is about the same subject as the background papers and e-mails.

- You should structure your response using the same guidance as the points below on the written assessment.

Assessment centre: general points

- If you pass the e-tray exercise then you will be invited to attend the assessment centre.
- Take a moment to congratulate yourself. You have succeeded in a process where the number of candidates has been pared down from well over 10,000 to under 1,000.
- Now put aside all self-congratulatory thoughts and get down to some serious work. You still have a significant series of obstacles to overcome. Begin by studying carefully the very detailed guide to the assessment centre found in the secure section of the Fast Stream website.
- The day may well start early, so ensure you arrive in good time. It is very unlikely that you will be admitted if you arrive late.
- It will be a long day and by the end of it you may well be flagging, but first and foremost try to enjoy it – or at least look as if you are!
- The attendees will be divided into groups and each group will undertake the various assignments at different times. For example, you may do the written assignment in the morning while others do it in the afternoon.
- A self-assessment form at the end of the day could well be part of your assessment – so answer it thoughtfully and be self-critical especially with respect to how you might improve your performance.
- Dress smartly but comfortably; a formal suit is not necessary but by all means wear one if you wish.

Written assignment
- The written assignment is completed on a PC so make sure that your keyboard skills are up to scratch.
- The examiners are looking to see how well you can structure an argument and examine a number of options,

recommending one. For this reason it is probably best not to use bullet points.

- Consider starting with a summary of what you say and then commit a paragraph on each of the options.
- State your reasons for not selecting each option as well as making it clear why you recommend your preferred selection.
- If appropriate, use illustrations to make your points.
- Rather than quoting from the background information, consider paraphrasing it or restating the passage in your own words.
- Demonstrate your ability at handling numerical information by offering clear, succinct restatements of relevant data in the background information.
- Cite reference sources.
- Be convincing while remaining impartial and objective.
- Adopt an elegant, fluid, readable style.
- Take care to use the correct grammar, spellings and punctuation.

Interview

- At the interview you are likely to face a panel of three, one of whom may well be an occupational psychologist, but don't let this bother you. You will find it a normal interview, so treat it as such.
- It's easy to say, but try not to allow nerves to get the better of you. The interviewers are not trying to find fault or catch you out, but to establish your true potential.
- Do read one of the many interview books, such as *Great Answers to Tough Interview Questions* by Martin Yates published by Kogan Page.
- Prepare for the usual competency questions. If you have done some of the thinking before the interview, this will help you deal with nerves.
- Be sure you are able to adapt your prepared response to reflect and answer follow-up questions.
- A good interview is first and foremost a conversation where there are mostly points of agreement.

- Be sure you have thought about why you want to be a civil servant, what you believe Fast Stream involves and why you have applied to join it.

Group exercise and presentations

- Identify from the background papers plenty of facts and figures to back up your case.
- Don't worry if your position is entirely different from everyone else's. The assessors are interested in how well you can make your case, not what case you are making.
- Do help ensure that everyone has a say and do show decisiveness and leadership qualities, but avoid adopting the role of chair.
- Make lots of eye contact and nod in agreement, but don't shake your head or demonstrate your disagreement through body language.
- Demonstrate that you can listen and have understood the significance of the contribution of others by modifying your position to take account of their comments.
- Consider making explicit reference to how you have modified your case to take into account the contributions of others. You can do this by, for example, offering supportive summaries of their contributions then adding a further relevant point of your own.
- Set out to make as good a case as you can for the view that you are representing.
- Don't start or get sucked into an argument; in the unlikely event that one occurs, do try to help make peace between the parties.
- Make sure you are enthusiastic even when discussing what might seem very mundane issues.
- If you do not have sufficient time to read all of the background papers, make absolutely sure you have sufficient evidence to back up what you plan to say. Include plenty of figures.
- Be constructive in your contributions and be supportive of others in your group.

- Keep your contributions to the point. If you refer to something not obviously significant to the discussion, be sure to spell out its relevance.
- Before you attend, review the competencies that are described as key to a successful Fast Stream candidate (see the website) and make sure that your contribution can be judged as representative of them.
- Be creative, but remember to back up all your points with facts and figures from the background material.

If you get in

- There are lots of really interesting Fast Stream jobs and some not so interesting, so take care over selecting your parent department.
- Be sure to take responsibility for your own development. If you find yourself in an undemanding role, then ask to be transferred to one in which you will learn more.
- When choosing a position, think about the area of work as well as the department. Select the area that interests you most; it might be, for example, the environment, European and overseas regional policy, constitutional or legal affairs, or economics and finance to name but a few.
- You should not expect to stay in any post for more than 18 months.

If like many, many others you fail

- Really very accomplished candidates fail the Fast Stream selection process so do not conclude that you are not capable of being a very good civil servant.
- Don't be put off. It is common for people to pass only at their third attempt or later. So plan a programme of revision, get down to some serious practice and apply again!
- Taking and failing the Fast Stream is the best possible practice you can obtain! So long as you remain as determined as before, you will definitely do better the next time.

- Sit down and write down your recollection of the process, and undertake some self-assessment of your performance. In particular, reflect honestly on how you might do better next time.

- Use the official feedback, which will give some indication of where you need to improve. Don't expect too much, though; many people are disappointed with its lack of detail.

- This feedback will be computer generated and restricted to broad areas of competency such as handling data and ideas, and working with colleagues.

- There are many other worthwhile entry points into the public sector and structured career paths. Many people, especially graduates, would benefit from realizing that the Fast Stream is not the only route into the Civil Service.

- Departments such as HM Revenue & Customs, HM Treasury and The Highways Agency run their own graduate recruitment scheme. There are also professional entry routes for many disciplines.

- If you join the Civil Service at a non-Fast Stream grade, after two years' service and with your managers support you can apply for the 'In-Service Fast Stream'. This is the accelerated promotion scheme designed for those who are already civil servants.

- The overall success rate for the 'In Service Fast Stream' is almost 50 per cent (source: the *Fast Stream Report 2005*).

- Consider reapplying after a few years' work in the private sector. You may well then succeed, as that experience will have helped develop many of the skills tested in the Fast Stream.

Practice for the Fast Stream

The competition is fierce. The Fast Stream usually attracts over 10,000 applicants a year and under 300 appointments are made. To succeed you will have to be very well prepared. If you are serious about wanting to join the programme, set about a significant timetable of preparation. Be prepared to concentrate on the areas in which you do least well. The assessors are looking for both a high score and a well-balanced score. To have any chance of success you have to score consistently well across all the criteria.

The bulk of the material in this and the next chapter is intended to provide practice material for the online tests. The data interpretation exercises will also help in preparing for the e-tray exercise. The chapter concludes with some exercises to help prepare for the assessment day.

The Fast Stream recruitment process is carefully explained on the website www.faststream.gov.uk It is vital that you study this site fully and ensure that you are totally familiar with the competencies tested and the nature of each challenge in the process. The Fast Stream is an intense competition and a major test of endurance. You will attempt a series of assessments, often against strict time constraints, over a number of hours. You really have to apply yourself if you are to show your true potential. When you have completed each assessment you should feel worn out; otherwise you cannot expect to stand out from the crowd.

The Fast Stream online tests

This section and the next chapter are intended to provide additional practice questions to supplement those available on the Fast Stream site. Further material is available in other Kogan Page publications including:

● *The Graduate Psychometric Test Workbook;*
● *How to Pass Graduate Psychometric Tests, 3rd edition;*
● *How to Pass Advanced Numeracy Tests;*
● *The Advanced Numeracy Tests Workbook;*
● *How to Pass Advanced Verbal Reasoning Tests* (to be published late 2007).

Ensure that you provide answers to all the questions in both of the online sub-tests. If you do not know the answer to a question, then eliminate as many incorrect answers as you can and then guess.

Warm-up questions for the data-interpretation test

In the real test you have 25 minutes to complete a block of 20 questions.

The test comprises tables of data or passages of information, each of which has associated questions. Five alternative answers are given, from which you must select the right one. Indicate your answer by writing the letter of the correct answer in the answer box. ·

It sometimes helps to look at the suggested answers before you attempt lengthy calculations, as you may be able to rule out some of the options and then estimate the correct answer by rounding sums up or down to more convenient figures.

Try the 30 practice questions below. Do not using a calculator. Aim to complete them in 25 minutes.

Data-interpretation test

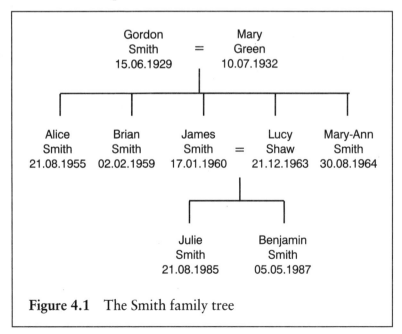

Figure 4.1   The Smith family tree

1.   How old will Brian be on 01.02.2004?

     A 44   B 45   C 46   D 47   E 48   F 49

                    Answer: [   ]

2.   What is the age difference between Alice and Julie?

     A 21 years   B 25 years   C 26 years   D 30 years
     E 32 years   F 34 years

                    Answer: [   ]

3.   Gordon died in an accident before Mary-Ann was born.
     Alice was only eight, Brian and James were both four.
     When did he die?

     A August 1963   B October 1963   C November 1963
     D January 1964   E May 1964   F June 1964

                    Answer: [   ]

4.   Julie and Alice share the same birthday. For presents one
     year Alice gives Julie a cheque and Julie presents her aunt
     with a bouquet of roses worth £15.00. Julie quickly calcu-
     lates that her aunt has spent 25 per cent more than she
     received. How much money did Julie gain?

     A £2.50   B £5.00   C £10.00   D £15.00   E £17.50
     F £20.00

                    Answer: [   ]

Table 4.1   2001 top-20 earners (taken as an average across the whole of each profession)

Rank	Occupation	Salary 2001 (£)	Salary 1991 (£)
1	General managers (large companies)	110,341	52,449
2	Barristers	78,549	30,813
3	Senior general administrators, Civil Service	61,993	39,944
4	Treasurers & company financial managers	59,121	25,692
5	Aircraft pilots	57,328	42,055
6	Managers in mining & energy industries	48,916	32,017
7	Doctors	48,235	30,822
8	Insurance underwriters, claims assessors	46,034	28,928
9	Management consultants	45,313	29,914
10	Judges and court officers	45,022	28,435
11	IT managers	43,268	27,440
12	Work study managers	42,867	26,099
13	Police officers (inspector and above)	41,984	30,660
14	Chemical engineers	40,926	26,657
15	Air, commodity & ship brokers	40,421	33,144
16	Solicitors	39,775	28,081
17	Marketing & sales managers	39,750	25,692
18	Personnel managers	37,216	25,187
19	Physicists, geologists & meteorologists	36,829	25,890
20	Air traffic planners & controllers	36,797	27,476

5. Which occupation showed the lowest percentage change between 1991 and 2001?

A Senior general administrators: Civil Service.
B Aircraft pilots.
C Doctors.
D Police officers (inspector and above).
E Air, commodity & ship brokers.
F Air traffic planners & controllers.

Answer:

6. What is the difference in average earnings between 1991 and 2001?

    A £14,961.50   B £15,649.10   C £16,591.40
    D £16,914.50   E £19,164.50   F £19,654.10

    Answer:

7. By what minimum percentage would air traffic planners and controllers have had to increase their 1991 wage to become top of the list in 2001?

    A 151.1   B 199.9   C 252.4   D 301.6   E 355.3
    F 410.8

    Answer:

8. Professional athletes earned £17,652 in 1991. If their earnings had increased by 166.3 per cent where would they have ranked in 2001?

    A 6th   B 7th   C 8th   D 9th   E 10th   F 11th

    Answer:

Table 4.2   Gross weekly earnings of full-time adult employees in Great Britain

| | Median gross weekly earnings (£) | | | |
	Manual men	Non-manual men	Manual women	Non-manual women
1986	163.4	219.4	101.1	131.5
1987	173.9	235.7	108.2	142.2
1988	188.0	259.7	115.6	157.1
1989	203.9	285.7	125.9	173.5
1990	221.3	312.1	137.3	191.8
1991	235.4	332.2	147.4	211.1
1992	250.7	353.4	156.6	227.6

9. Which year saw the greatest increase in earnings for manual women workers?

   A 1986–87   B 1987–88   C 1988–89   D 1989–90
   E 1990–91   F 1991–92

   Answer: [   ]

10. How much more must non-manual women workers earn to bring them in line with men in similar occupations in 1992?

    A £23.10   B £71.00   C £94.10   D £102.70
    E £125.80   F £196.80

    Answer: [   ]

11. By what percentage have the earnings of non-manual men workers increased between 1988 and 1992?

    A 36.1%   B 42.5%   C 45.6%   D 49.7%   E 54.8%
    F 61.1%

    Answer: [   ]

12. What was the average weekly wage difference between manual and non-manual men workers between 1986 and 1992?

    A £79.80   B £80.23   C £81.40   D £81.90   E £82.20
    F £83.60

    Answer: [   ]

Table 4.3   UK government expenditure on education in real terms, by type

Sector	£ million		
	1970–1	1980–1	1991–2
Schools			
Nursery	58	114	
Primary	4,713	5,886	
Secondary	5,523	7,754	8,287
Special	442	917	1,280
Higher, further and adult education*	2,884	3,517	3,734
Polytechnics and Colleges Funding Council	–	–	993
Universities	2,325	2,698	2,668
Other education expenditure	706	1,027	1,394
Total	**16,651**	**21,913**	**25,976**
Related education expenditure	2,727	2,678	2,995
VAT on above expenditure	2,132	2,705	5,070
Total expenditure	**21,510**	**27,296**	**34,041**
Total expenditure as a percentage of GDP	**5.2**	**5.5**	**5.1**

*Includes fees for polytechnics and colleges transferred to the Polytechnics and Colleges Funding Council in April 1989

13. If the fees had not been transferred to the Polytechnics and Colleges Funding Council in April 1989, how much would higher, further and adult education have received in 1991?

   A £993 million   B £3,734 million   C £4,727 million
   D £6,401 million   E £10,135 million
   F £11,128 million

   Answer: [   ]

14. What was the percentage increase in expenditure on secondary education between 1970 and 1991?

A 6.9%   B 40.4%   C 24.6%   D 31.3%   E 45.5%
F 50.0%

Answer:

15. What was the total GDP for 1991?

A £34,041 million   B £58,725 million
C £509,333 million   D £568,059 million
E £667,471 million   F £680,820 million

Answer:

16. What was the rate of VAT in 1980?

A 7.5%   B 11.0%   C 12.5%   D 14.0%   E 15.0%
F 17.5%

Answer:

Table 4.4   Liverpool tides

Date	High water AM Time	m	PM Time	m	Low water AM Time	m	PM Time	m	Sun Rise	Set	Moon Rise	Set
14.04	0001	9.2	1216	9.3	0634	1.1	1853	1.0	0530	1856	1933	0229
15.04	0030	9.1	1247	9.2	0707	1.1	1924	1.1	0527	1858	2046	0304
16.04	0100	9.0	1318	9.0	0741	1.3	1956	1.4	0525	1859	2144	0350
17.04	0131	8.8	1350	8.7	0814	1.6	2028	1.8	0523	1901	2228	0450
18.04	0203	8.5	1428	8.3	0848	2.0	2102	2.3	0520	1903	2259	0558
19.04	0242	8.1	1516	7.9	0927	2.4	2144	2.7	0518	1905	2323	0712
20.04	0337	7.7	1624	7.4	1022	2.8	2249	3.1	0516	1907	2341	0826

Table 4.4 shows the high and low tides at Liverpool for one week during April. Information is provided for the time of the tide, its height, and the sun and moon times. Note: all times shown are GMT.

17. What is the range in tide height throughout the week?

A 1.0 m   B 7.7 m   C 8.1 m   D 8.3 m   E 9.2 m
F 9.3 m

Answer: [   ]

18. Which period has the lowest mean tide?

A Morning   B Afternoon   C Both the same
D Cannot be calculated

Answer: [   ]

19. How many hours of sunlight are there on 17 April?

A 14 hr 38 m   B 14 hr 28 m   C 14 hr 18 m
D 13 hr 78 m   E 13 hr 58 m   F 13 hr 38 m

Answer: [   ]

20. Southport lies 35 minutes behind Liverpool. What time was the morning high tide at Southport on 14 April?

A There was no morning tide   B 00.26   C 00.36
D 11.26   E 11.41   F 12.26

Answer: [   ]

Table 4.5   Performance and value of investments

Investment	%	$ value
UK shares	14.6	1,375,200
US shares	9.8	1,976,400
Japanese shares	1.6	406,400
Nickel, silver and gold	62.1	486,300
Crude oil	1.3	2,000,000
UK high risk	(0.9)	700,000
US long term	(0.9)	900,000

Table 4.5 shows the performance of investments in 2006, percentage change on 2005 (in brackets) and $ value of investment end of 2006.

21. Find the median percentage change.
     A 87.8   B 12.5   C 1.6   D 1.3   E –0.9

     Answer:

22. What is the range of the percentage values?
     A 61.2   B 12.5   C 62.1   D 1.3   E 63

     Answer:

23. Which of the suggested answers most closely represents the increase in value in the investment in Japanese shares since 2005?
     A $6,400   B $4,064   C $6,502.4   D $4,000   E $6,000

     Answer:

24. What was the highest sum made on a single investment in 2006?

A $200,779   B $193,637   C $176,400   D $175,200
E $174,000

Answer: [   ]

25. If at the end of 2006 the sum remaining in the UK high risk was moved for a period of three years to a safer investment paying compounded interest at 3 per cent per year, which of the suggested formulas would correctly calculate the sum earned during that term?

A 693,700 × 3 × 3 – 693,700.
B 700,000 × (1.03)3.
C 693,700 × (1.03)3 – 693,700.
D 700,000 × 3 × 0.3.
E 693,700 × (1.03)3.
F 700,000 × (1.03)3 – 700,000.

Answer: [   ]

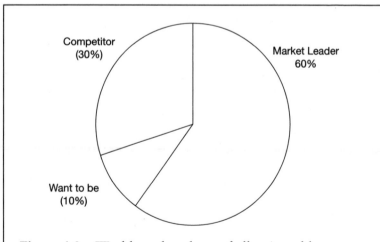

Figure 4.2   World market share of all units sold

Table 4.6   The business model 2006

Per unit retail price	$9.99
Retailers' commission	$5.49
Cost of sales (per unit):	
Material costs	$1.20
Licence fees	$0.45
Distribution	$0.50
Direct sales team	$0.50
Overheads	$1.50

Figure 4.2 shows the world market shares in sales of the latest fashion 'must have' manufactured by three companies: Market Leader, Competitor and Want to Be. Table 4.6 shows the business model on which all sales are based.

26. Market Leader plans to use its purchasing power to reduce costs and thereby triple the net profit on each unit. This represents what percentage increase over the business model?

A 100%   B 200%   C 300%   D 400%

Answer: [   ]

27. If Want to Be operates according to the business model and sells 2 million units, what net profit would it report (net profit = retail price − all cost of sales)?

A $7,000   B $70,000,000   C $70,000   D $7,000,000
E $700,000

Answer: [   ]

28. Competitor experiences production problems and the probability of a unit being faulty is an unacceptable 0.1. Estimate the chance of you buying a unit manufactured by Competitor that turns out to be faulty.

    A 0.02   B 0.03   C 0.04   D 0.05   E 0.06

    Answer: [   ]

29. If Want to Be sells 2 million units, which of the suggested answers is the best estimate of the mean for sales across all three manufacturers?

    A 5.5   B 6.6   C 7.7   D 8.8   E 9.9

    Answer: [   ]

30. If the business model had existed for four years and the retail price has increased at 5 per cent per annum since then, what was the retail price in 2002 (give your answer to the nearest cent)?

    A $8.25   B $8.24   C $8.23   D $8.22   E $8.21

    Answer: [   ]

Warm-up questions for the verbal test

Allow yourself 20 minutes to complete the following 40 questions. They comprise a passage and a group of statements that relate to the passage. Your task is to decide from the information in the passage whether each statement is true, false or it is impossible to tell. Indicate your answer by writing the letter of the correct answer, A–C, in the answer box.

You should avoid relying on your own specialist knowledge or opinions to decide on the answer and rely instead on the information contained in the passage. What it does not mean is that you should be like some Cartesian and start to question everything. You need to arrive at a sensible balance and not apply too strict or inflexible a test of proof. It is important that you learn to pick up clues from the wording of the question or statement. If, for example the question refers to 'a valid inference' or 'a premise', or asks 'is it necessarily the case' then by all means put on your logicians hat and apply strict criteria as to what can be deduced. However, if the question asks, for example, 'is it reasonable', 'on the balance of probability', 'might the author', then adjust your criterion accordingly and be prepared to apply judgement rather than strict logic.

If you are concerned about this style of question, then take heart from the fact that practice will make a big difference to your approach and performance in such verbal tests. Set aside the necessary time, get hold of sufficient practice questions, and allow yourself to become familiar with the attention to detail and the judgement calls these questions demand. Books on the General Management Attainment Test (GMAT – the test you must pass to get into the world's top graduate business schools) have loads of practice questions of this type.

Practise on the following examples. Remember the advice in tips and insights that some people find it best to read each passage twice, then reread the relevant part for each question.

Verbal test

Passage 1

An underground railway system is made up of five lines of equal length, all of which run in completely straight lines. The blue line runs north–south and intersects with the red line that runs east–west. The green line runs from southeast to northwest and intersects the red line east of the blue line. The yellow line runs from the northeast and intersects the blue line north of the red line. The grey line runs parallel to the green line, and intersects the blue line south of the red line.

1. The angle between the red and blue line at their point of intersection is 90 degrees.

    A True   B False   C Impossible to say

    Answer:

2. If the grey line were to intersect the red line it would do so west of the green line.

    A True   B False   C Impossible to say

    Answer:

3. The green line intersects the blue line east of the inter-section between the yellow line and the blue line.

    A True   B False   C Impossible to say

    Answer:

4.   The easternmost point of the green line is farther east than the easternmost point of the red line.

A True   B False   C Impossible to say

Answer: [   ]

Passage 2

The financial markets are seeking high yields and safe havens, which should boost the Australian and New Zealand dollar, but the Asian currencies have firmed versus the dollar too. Economic growth in East Asia appears to be on a sound footing but the yen's recent strengthening is not regarded as sustainable. Interest rates in the eurozone and UK are unlikely to move for the next few months. These rates are likely to remain unchanged for as much as a year, and then any rise is likely to be small.

5.   A rate decrease is expected in the eurozone shortly.

A True   B False   C Impossible to say

Answer: [   ]

6.   The yen is expected to weaken.

A True   B False   C Impossible to say

Answer: [   ]

7.   New Zealand's currency will remain aligned with the Australian currency.

A True   B False   C Impossible to say

Answer: [   ]

Passage 3

In a league of teams, a win scores two points, and a draw scores one point. Team 1 has four more points than Team 2, which has seven fewer points than Team 3. Team 4 has won more games than Team 1 and has lost no games. Team 5, on 17 points, is five points ahead of Team 4. Team 6 has four more points than Team 2. All teams have played the same number of games.

8. Team 4 has more points than Team 1.

    A True   B False   C Impossible to say

    Answer: [   ]

9. Team 6 has more points than Team 3.

    A True   B False   C Impossible to say

    Answer: [   ]

10. Team 2 is bottom of the league.

    A True   B False   C Impossible to say

    Answer: [   ]

Passage 4

The terms 'psychometric tests' and 'psychological testing' are used interchangeably to describe tools which are essentially sophisticated devices designed to measure individual differences in a number of areas such as intelligence and ability. If used appropriately, tests can enhance decision making and enable managers to develop more informed and accurate forecasts of an individual's potential. To achieve this it is essential that the test is integrated into the decision-making process. Even the best tests available are only as good as the process of which they form a part, and flawed decisions can still be made.

11. A psychometric test is the single best predictor of likely job performance.

    A True   B False   C Impossible to say

    Answer: [   ]

12. Psychological tests are most effective as tools to predict individual performance when integrated into the decision-making process.

    A True   B False   C Impossible to say

    Answer: [   ]

13. The principal point of the passage can be summed up as the assertion that the ability to measure individual differences allows a manager to forecast an individual's potential.

    A True   B False   C Impossible to say

    Answer: [   ]

Passage 5

During a 14-day holiday which starts on a Sunday, there are three days where the sky is clear all day. On the 11 days when there is some cloud, it rains on four different days. On one occasion it rains on consecutive days. On two occasions the sky is clear all day after it has rained on the day before. It rains on both of the Saturdays, one Friday and one Wednesday.

14. The days of the week on which it rains consecutively are a Friday and a Saturday.

A True   B False   C Impossible to say

Answer: [   ]

15. The sky is clear on at least one Sunday.

A True   B False   C Impossible to say

Answer: [   ]

16. The highest number of consecutive days without rain is six.

A True   B False   C Impossible to say

Answer: [   ]

Passage 6

A stakeholder pension plan is a simple and tax-efficient way of saving specifically for your retirement. All contributions qualify for tax relief at the highest rate you pay, and growth is free of UK income tax and capital gains tax (the tax on dividends from UK companies cannot be reclaimed). With a few exceptions anyone can pay up to £3,600 gross a year regardless of their age or employment status. Over this level further amounts can be invested based on your earnings in the current tax year or any of the previous five tax years and your age. So, for example, those aged between 46 and 50 years of age can invest up to 25 per cent of their earnings, while those aged up to 35 can invest 17.5 per cent. In general the older the worker, the greater a percentage he or she is allowed to invest. Savers can increase or reduce their contributions at any time, or make one-off payments within the overall limits determined by their age and earnings.

17. You will be able to invest more than £3,600 a year into your stakeholder plan if you meet the age requirement.

    A True   B False   C Impossible to say

    Answer: [   ]

18. Someone who is 27 years of age can invest £5,250 a year of his/her salary of £30,000.

    A True   B False   C Impossible to say

    Answer: [   ]

19. If you pay tax at the higher rate of 40 per cent then your contributions will qualify for 40 per cent tax relief.

    A True   B False   C Impossible to say

    Answer: [   ]

Passage 7

For sale is an exceptional property overlooking the marketplace with a triple-aspect reception room commanding views across the popular area. The property is accessed via its own entrance on the ground floor and is arranged over the first, second and third floors of a period property. It comprises approximately 2,000 sq feet of living space. On the second floor are both the bedrooms, of which the master bedroom measures some 18 feet in length. On the third floor is a spectacular open plan kitchen/family room with a raised dining area and wrought iron spiral staircase affording access to a roof terrace. Underground parking is available by separate agreement.

20. All the bedrooms are on the floor below the kitchen.

A True   B False   C Impossible to say

Answer: [   ]

21. The reception room is 18 feet in length with commanding views of the marketplace.

A True   B False   C Impossible to say

Answer: [   ]

22. The reception room is on the first floor.

A True   B False   C Impossible to say

Answer: [   ]

Passage 8

The term 'operating environment' refers to the interaction of an information system (typically a computer) with its user. The means of communication between the system, its hardware and software, and the user is called the user interface. The term 'software' can be used to describe both systems software and applications software. The first of these controls the computer's operating systems; the second relates to the user-related programmes. The user interface is also called the human–computer interface. Ideally it should be as easy to use as possible, so that the users do not have to study instruction manuals. The interface consists of, for example, cursors, prompts, icons and menus. Prompts can be either visual or audible. Interfaces can be either command driven, menu driven or graphical. Command-driven interfaces are fast to use once you have learnt the commands, which are inputted through a keyboard. Menu-driven interfaces are much more user friendly, and can be inputted with either a mouse or keyboard.

23. A keyboard is an example of a command interface.

A True   B False   C Impossible to say

Answer: [   ]

24. Applications software is user related.

A True   B False   C Impossible to say

Answer: [   ]

25. The human–computer interface is a means of communication between the system, its hardware, software and the user.

A True   B False   C Impossible to say

Answer: [   ]

Passage 9

Kinematics is the branch of mathematics that deals with the motion of a particle in terms of displacement, velocity and acceleration, without considering the forces that may be required to cause the motion. For motion in a straight line, the distinction between distance and displacement is only that displacement may be positive or negative to indicate direction, whereas distance is always taken as positive. The same point can be made about speed and velocity. Velocity in a straight line may be positive or negative, depending on the direction, whereas speed is always positive. Kinematics can be contrasted with the subject of dynamics, which is concerned with the motion of a particle in response to forces that act on it.

26. Negative values can be used to indicate direction for both velocity and displacement.

A True   B False   C Impossible to say

Answer:

27. In dynamics speed is always attributed a positive value.

A True   B False   C Impossible to say

Answer:

28. Kinematics is concerned with the motion of a particle in a straight line but does not concern itself with the forces that act on the particle.

A True   B False   C Impossible to say

Answer:

Passage 10

A depression is an area of low barometric pressure, which is usually responsible for periods of unsettled weather and often accompanied by strong winds. Depressions occur most frequently in middle and high latitudes. (The most severe storms occur in the low latitudes but these tropical revolving storms must be classified differently from a depression because of the sheer violence they unleash.) Depressions in the northern hemisphere generate winds in an anticlockwise direction, while in the southern hemisphere the winds generated blow in the opposite direction. Most depressions move at speeds up to 40 miles per hour. They last about three to five days and gradually slow down as the low barometric pressure fills. The wind strengths are reported on synoptic charts by the closeness of the isobar lines: the closer the lines, the stronger the wind strengths. The approach of a depression can be forecast by a fall in barometric pressure and by cloud formations.

29. Someone with a map of the world could establish from the passage that depressions in Australia generate winds in a clockwise direction.

A True   B False   C Impossible to say

Answer: [   ]

30. If a depression passes directly over a town, the wind direction shifts through a total of 180 degrees.

A True   B False   C Impossible to say

Answer: [   ]

31. If you point your face directly into the wind of a depression in the northern hemisphere, your right ear will point towards the centre of the depression.

A True   B False   C Impossible to say

Answer: [   ]

Passage 11

Both sides of a high street are made up of two identical rows of 20 uninterrupted shops exactly opposite each other. There is only one example of each type of shop. Between the pharmacist and the newsagent there are two other shops. Directly across the road from the newsagent is an off-licence. The optician is next door to the insurance broker and two shops away from the off-licence. The pedestrian crossing outside the pharmacist crosses over to the post office, with a clothes shop on one side and butcher on the other. The bus stop is directly across the road from the optician.

32. The pharmacist is on the same side of the road as the insurance broker.

    A True   B False   C Impossible to say

    Answer:

33. The bus stop is on the same side of the road as the pharmacist.

    A True   B False   C Impossible to say

    Answer:

34. The optician is next door to the butcher.

    A True   B False   C Impossible to say

    Answer:

Passage 12

Begin laying the wooden laminate floor in a left-hand corner, with wedges between the boards and the wall, and with the tongues facing into the room. Start the second row with the piece left over from the first row. Leave at least 50 cm between end joints. Apply glue along the whole of the upper side of the groove, on both the long and short sides of the boards. Tap the boards immediately together using a mallet and tapping block. Fit the skirting boards.

35. You would expect the last piece of flooring to be laid in a right hand corner.

    A True   B False   C Impossible to say

    Answer:

36. Starting the second row with the leftover piece will help ensure that adjoining end pieces are unaligned.

    A True　B False　C Impossible to say

    Answer:

37. The short end of the board is its end.

    A True　B False　C Impossible to say

    Answer:

Passage 13

It takes James nine minutes to get to the meeting, although he sets off five minutes later than Helen. It takes Steve longer to get to the meeting than Helen, but not as long as it takes James. It takes Pete and Sarah the same length of time to get to the meeting, but they do not set off at the same time. Sarah and James do set off at the same time. Steve and Pete arrive at the same time, just after Helen. Richard has to travel farther than anyone else.

38. It takes Steve nine minutes to travel to the meeting.

    A True　B False　C Impossible to say

    Answer:

39. James arrives at the meeting after Helen.

    A True　B False　C Impossible to say

    Answer:

40. Richard would have to set off before everyone else in order to arrive first.

    A True   B False   C Impossible to say

    Answer: [   ]

Preparing for the assessment centre

If you receive an invitation to the assessment centre then you have made it through to something like the top 1,000 candidates (across the combined Fast Stream options) and you should feel justly content. You should also appreciate that you are soon to be subjected to an entirely different sort of assessment from the one so far. This is because now that the numbers are more manageable the service will start examining you more as an individual than as a statistic.

On the assessment day it is essential that you present yourself as a candidate fit for the Fast Stream. Attend with the intention of making every word your say or write sound like one typical of the perfect Fast Streamer.

Begin your preparations early. Start by reflecting on the competencies and qualities that make an ideal Fast Stream candidate, which are described at various points on the Fast Stream website. You need to explore the meaning of these descriptions and build up your own impression of the qualities the ideal candidate would have.

To help get you thinking and build your impression of the ideal candidate, consider the list of qualities shown below, and prioritize them in terms of whether you consider they are essential or desirable for the role. They are not from any official source, nor are they a complete list of the competencies a Fast Streamer should possess, just some issues that it might be helpful for you to think over.

Analyse problems in a logical and well-organized way.

Essential	Desirable

Co-operatively develop practical solutions to problems.

Essential	Desirable

Show clarity of vision in the assessment of intricate circumstances.

Essential	Desirable

Provide clear direction in the management of change.

Essential	Desirable

Identify appropriate principal goal(s) for a complex assignment.

Essential	Desirable

Assign and communicate roles to each member of a team.

Essential	Desirable

Offer compelling arguments.

Essential	Desirable

Interact creatively and positively with colleagues and representatives of outside organizations.

Essential	Desirable

Show diplomacy, integrity and diligence.

Essential	Desirable

Anticipate future trends, problems or opportunities and devise suitable strategies.

Essential	Desirable

Win support for new initiatives.

Essential	Desirable

Negotiate effectively with representatives from a broad church of interests, backgrounds and groups.

Essential	Desirable

Demonstrate a mastery of numerical data.

Essential	Desirable

This is not an exhaustive list so add other items as you consider fit.

Once you have formed a view of the qualities held by the ideal Fast Streamer then set about making sure that an assessor will attribute these qualities to you. Do this by:

1. Making sure that you can illustrate a time when you have portrayed each of the qualities and use these to inform your responses in the interview.
2. Reflecting on how you might conduct yourself in a group exercise so that an assessor might attribute these qualities to you.
3. Devising some broad strategies that are symptomatic of these competencies and work out how you might adopt them in a written assessment.

Practice tests for the Fast Stream

This chapter presents a practice Fast Stream test. As in the case of the real test, there are verbal and numerical sub-tests. The time allowed, number of questions and competencies tested are similar to the online Fast Stream tests. Obviously, unlike the real test, this one is not online but otherwise treat it as if it were the real thing and take it under test-like conditions. Find a quiet space where you can work uninterrupted. Sit the two sub-tests one after the other allowing no more than a five-minute break. Try to realize your very best score.

Remember, if you are to show your true potential, you really have to go for it and apply yourself. Make this kind of commitment under practice conditions that simulate the real test. That will help you perfect your exam technique and maximize the benefit of practice.

When you have finished mark your answers and go over any questions you got wrong.

Do not read too much into your score. This is a practice test not the real thing, and is intended only as a source of practice. It is not possible to state a definitive pass mark but you should not be content with anything less than a very good score. So make an objective assessment of your performance and set about a programme of revision to address any area of underperformance. If necessary be prepared to undertake quite a significant programme of revision. Keep practising until you really excel at these sorts of test. You can source hundreds more further practice questions in the books listed in Chapter 4.

Practice test 1: data interpretation

This test comprises 20 questions. Allow yourself 25 minutes to complete it. Indicate your answer by writing the letter of the correct answer in the answer box

Be sure to stop as soon as the 25 minutes is over.

You may use a calculator but try not to waste time by relying on it too much. Use one without many functions as this is the sort provided by Fast Stream – then the practice will be more realistic. If you have time to spare at the end of the test, go back over your answers to check that they are correct.

Use rough paper for working out.

Do not turn the page until you are ready to begin.

Data interpretation

Situation 1

Addison, Baldock, Clark, Dickinson, Edwards, Fitch, Gordon, Humphreys, Isaacs, Jordan, Keith, Lloyd, Milton, Newton and Orwell all take extra woodwind lessons on a Tuesday. Using their initials, Mrs Richards, their peripatetic teacher, has produced the monthly timetable shown in Table 5.1.

Each child pays £5.00 per lesson. However, Addison, Dickinson, Edwards, Fitch and Keith are currently subsidized by the school, and pay £2.50. Addison and Edwards will begin paying the full rate from 14 November.

Table 5.1   Monthly timetable

Date	5/11	12/11	19/11	26/11
08.30	A	H	F	N
09.00	O	I	K	D
09.30	C	A	H	F
10.00	M	O	I	K
10.30	E	C	A	H
11.00	L	M	O	I
11.30	G	E	C	A
12.00	J	L	M	O
12.30	B	G	E	C
13.00	N	J	L	M
13.30	D	B	G	E
14.00	F	N	J	L
14.30	K	D	B	G
15.00	H	F	N	J
15.30	I	K	D	B

1. On average, which are Mrs Richards' most profitable lessons?

   A   08.30; 09.00; 10.00; 11.00.
   B   09.30; 10.00; 12.00; 12.30.
   C   11.00; 12.00; 12.30; 13.00.
   D   13.30; 14.00; 15.00; 15.30.

   Answer:

2. When examination time approaches, Mrs Richards offers extra tuition after school at £6.00 per half hour, or £3.50 per pupil if a lesson is shared. Music exams start in December. Clark, Gordon and Humphreys have requested extra lessons. Clark and Gordon both play the saxophone and will share their lesson. Extra tuition starts on 19 November. How much money will Mrs Richards be earning in this week?

   A £75.50   B £80.50   C £81.50   D £83.50

   Answer:

3. Owing to sickness among many of her students, Mrs Richards has to reorganize her timetable for the week of 26 November. The altered lessons are as follows: Edwards at 14.30; Gordon at 10.00; Jordan at 12.00; Keith at 11.00; and Orwell at 13.30. Baldock and Isaacs are away sick. From 13.00 her appointments are as follows:

   A M-A-K-E   B M-I-K-E   C M-O-C-K-E-D   D M-O-L-E

   Answer:

4. The school concert is planned for 22 December. Every student is given five tickets at £4.00 each to sell to friends and family. £212.00 and a number of unsold tickets are returned. Jordan did not sell any, whereas Addison, Dickinson, Fitch, Keith, Lloyd and Newton sold all theirs. What is the average number of tickets sold per student?

   A 2.80   B 3.00   C 3.50   D 4.00

   Answer:

Situation 2

InterSun Ltd has slashed the price of holidays to the Canary Islands. In Table 5.2 its new rates are shown compared with its old fares:

Table 5.2   InterSun Ltd holidays

| Departure dates | | Destination | Board | Price per person/week | |
From	To			Old	New
1 July	14 July	Fuerteventura	SC	£150	£125
		Gran Canaria	SC	£165	£130
		Lanzarote	HB	£180	£140
		Tenerife	HB	£200	£150
15 July	28 July	Fuerteventura	SC	£200	£150
		Gran Canaria	SC	£215	£160
		Lanzarote	HB	£230	£180
		Tenerife	HB	£250	£200
29 July	31 August	Fuerteventura	SC	£250	£200
		Gran Canaria	SC	£275	£225
		Lanzarote	HB	£325	£275
		Tenerife	HB	£350	£300

5. A customer wants to visit Lanzarote for two weeks between 7 and 21 July. How much will he or she save?

   A £80   B £90   C £100   D £110

   Answer:

6. Airport tax increases on 10 August to £65.00 per person, from an original £42.00 per person. InterSun Ltd has already sold 6,731 holidays for this period and cannot now introduce the new charge to these customers. What are its losses?

   A £154,813   B £154,956   C £164,765   D £165,814

   Answer:

7.   Self-catering (SC) holidays offer a further 25 per cent reduction on prices for holidays in Fuerteventura during August. What is the total saving on the original price for a two-week holiday starting 21 July?

A £187.50   B£175.00   C £160.50   D £150.00

Answer: [   ]

8.   In August, which destination has the greatest percentage increase over the late July rates?

A Fuerteventura   B Gran Canaria   C Lanzarote   D Tenerife

Answer: [   ]

Situation 3

Kash Ltd offer personal loans at 8.9 per cent APR. Table 5.3 below shows the repayments over various monthly instalments either with payment protection cover (PP) or without payment protection cover (W/O) for loans between £5,000 and £20,000. Payment protection cover ensures continued loan repayments in the event of involuntary unemployment, illness or disability. All repayments are fixed for the entire period of the loan and guaranteed never to rise.

Table 5.3   Kash Ltd

Loan £	12 months		24 months		36 months		48 months		60 months	
	W/O	PP	W/O	PP	W/O	PP	W/O	PP	W/O	PP
20,000	1,745.26	1,865.77	909.97	999.94	632.22	704.25	793.85	569.86	411.23	482.21
17,500	1,527.10	1,632.55	796.22	875.03	553.19	616.22	432.12	498.63	359.83	421.94
15,000	1,308.95	1,399.33	682.48	750.03	474.16	528.19	371.39	427.40	308.42	361.65
12,500	1,090.79	1,166.11	568.73	625.02	395.14	440.16	308.65	356.16	257.02	301.38
10,000	872.63	932.89	454.98	500.01	316.11	352.13	246.92	284.93	205.62	241.11
8,000	698.10	746.30	363.99	400.02	252.89	281.70	197.54	227.95	164.49	192.88
6,000	523.58	559.73	272.99	300.01	189.66	211.27	148.15	170.95	123.37	144.66
5,000	436.32	466.45	227.49	250.01	158.05	176.06	123.46	142.46	102.81	120.55

Note: customers who do not satisfy Kash Ltd's normal scoring criteria may be offered a loan with an APR of up to 4 per cent above the typical rates shown. An additional variable administration fee will also be payable; information concerning that is available upon request.

9.   How much will a customer repay Kash Ltd for a loan of £12,500 borrowed over 48 months (with payment protection cover)?

A £13,676.64   B £14,815.20   C £15,421.20
D £17,095.68   E £18,505.20   F £20,515.20

Answer:

10.   Kash Ltd offers a repayment plan of £154.21 over 60 months for a loan of £7,500. This is a saving of £598.80 on a competitor, Loans-R-Us Ltd, which offers its customers an APR of 11.9 per cent over the same period. How much in total do customers of Loans-R-Us Ltd repay?

A £8,098.80   B £9,252.60   C £9,851.40   D £9,993.50
E £10,156.00   F £10,512.80

Answer:

11.   Mr Patel requests a loan of £10,000. Which of the following is his cheapest form of repayment?

A 12 months PP   B 24 months W/O   C 24 months PP
D 36 months W/O   E 36 months PP   F 48 months W/O

Answer:

12.   Unfortunately Mr Fox has a very poor credit rating and Kash Ltd has offered him an APR 3 per cent above the typical rate for a loan of £5,000. What are his monthly repayments (without payment protection cover) over 36 months?

A 164.40   B 176.06   C 185.45   D 187.60   E 191.23
F Cannot be calculated

Answer:

Situation 4

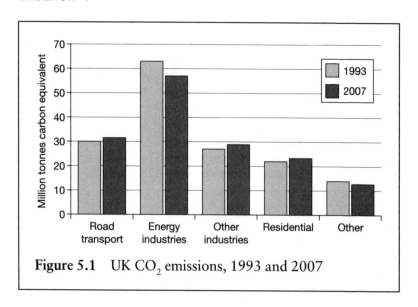

Figure 5.1   UK CO_2 emissions, 1993 and 2007

13. Which pair of bars saw the greatest percentage increase over
    the 14 year period?

    A Road transport   B Energy industries   C Other industries
    D Residential   E Other

    Answer:

14. Express in its simplest form the ratio between emissions in 1993
    for energy transport and other industries.

    A 5:3   B 6:3   C 7:3   D 8:3

    Answer:

15. If CO_2 emissions from road transport prior to 1993 had increased by 10 per cent per annum, in what year would emissions from road transport amount to 20 million tonnes?

    A 1991   B 1990   C 1989   D 1988   E 1997

    Answer: [   ]

16. By what percentage would the UK's overall 2007 CO_2 emissions fall if government road pricing and energy efficient homes policies succeeded in cutting road transport and residential emissions by 50 per cent?

    A 0–5%   B 5–10%   C 10–15%   D 15–20%   E 20–25%

    Answer: [   ]

Situation 5

Table 5.4   Rate of exchange and percentage change in that rate

Currency	Currency: Euro rate yesterday	Today's rate as % change on yesterday
Peso	1:0.055	4%
Rupiah	1:0.00084	–6%
Yuan	1:0.099	8%
Balit	1:0.021	–2%
Ringgit	1:0.022	?

17. If today's exchange rate for the balit:euro is 1:0.01995, what was the percentage change on yesterday's rate?

    A 5%   B 3%   C 1%   D –3%   E –5%

    Answer: [   ]

18. What is the peso:euro rate today?

    A 1:0.0572   B 1:0.0563   C 1:0.0539   D 1:0.0528

    Answer: [   ]

19. What is today's rate for the rupiah:euro?

    A 1:0.0008904   B 1:0.0008196   C 1:0.0007896
    D 1:0.0006986

    Answer: [   ]

20. If issued in response to the change in the rate of the yuan, which statement has most credence, given that economic zones export dependency?

    A   The change will fuel inflation within the yuan zone.
    B   Outflows of money seeking higher returns are causing the change.
    C   The international headlines of mass street protests in the yuan zone are causing the currency's fluctuation.
    D   The change will help hold down inflation within the Yuan zone.

    Answer: [   ]

End of test.

Practice test 2: the verbal test

This test comprises 40 questions to be completed in 20 minutes. Use it to practise making judgements and correct inferences. Indicate your answer by writing the letter of the correct answer in the answer box

Be sure to stop as soon as the 20 minutes are over.

Practise the recommended strategy of reading each passage twice and then referring back to the passage to answer the specific point raised in the question. If you have time to spare at the end of the test, go back over your answers to check you are happy with them.

Do not turn the page until you are ready to begin.

Verbal test

Passage 1

Widespread help from parents and family members generally has always cast doubt on the value of examinations in which home-completed assignments contribute to the grade awarded. Between 20 and 60 per cent of marks generally come from such coursework. Most students believe that coursework is a fairer method of assessment when compared with 'all or nothing' exams; however, they also admit that it is 'all too easy to cheat'. A review of the extent of cheating found overwhelming evidence of widespread abuse by students, teachers and parents. Incredibly, 1 in 10 parents admitted to doing assignments for their children. Teachers admitted to giving students 'too much help'. But the greatest concern arises because of the internet. A whole host of sites now exist that offer model essays and examples of coursework awarded top grades for a small fee (or even for free). Most of these sites carry requests that users should not submit the material as their own, but there is no attempt to ensure that this request is respected and there is much evidence of a plagiarism free-for-all of internet-obtained material.

1. In the passage it is concluded that the internet has made the policing of coursework impossible.

    A True   B False   C Cannot tell

    Answer:

2. The extent of the contribution from home-completed assignments to the grade awarded can be best described as:

    A Significant   B Serious   C Noteworthy   D A scandal
    E There is insufficient information to answer the question correctly

    Answer:

3.   The author relies on which one of the following to make his claims:

   A   Examples or analogies.
   B   Deductive argument.
   C   The drawing of comparative assertions.
   D   The findings of a investigative study.
   E   The results of an experimental investigation.

Answer: [   ]

4.   It is reasonable to infer from the passage that widespread help from parents and siblings has raised serious questions about the credibility of vocational qualifications.

   A True   B False   C Cannot tell

Answer: [   ]

Passage 2

A study of the benefits of a family of cholesterol-lowering drugs used in the treatment of heart attacks has shown that while the greatest benefits are enjoyed by those at greatest risk of a vascular event, every person at risk can gain considerable benefits from the treatment. These findings have led to calls that it should be offered to anybody at risk of a heart attack or stroke. It has long been known that the treatment, if administered daily to the group most at risk of an attack, sees that risk cut by a third. At present doctors prescribe the treatment only once they have considered a number of factors, including cholesterol level, blood pressure, body-fat levels and whether the patient smokes. The new evidence suggests that patients with less than very high levels of cholesterol will also experience a significant drop in their cholesterol levels and a consequently lower risk of a vascular event. In fact the study concludes that the benefits of the treatment are directly proportional to the size of the reduction in cholesterol levels that might be achieved, and not the level at which the intervention begins.

5. A factor that gave rise to the call for the treatment to be offered to everyone at risk of a heart attack or stroke was the realization that not every person at risk can gain considerable benefits from the treatment.

    A True   B False   C Cannot tell

    Answer: [   ]

6. Which of these statements, if true, would most weaken the claim that patients with less than very high levels of cholesterol will also experience a significant drop in their cholesterol levels and a consequent much lower risk of a vascular event?

    A   The largest benefits from the treatment are seen among those at greatest risk of a vascular event, and those with less than very high levels of cholesterol are not at greatest risk.
    B   Unfortunately, the best results from the treatment can only be obtained when the treatment is customized to the individual patient's cholesterol levels; achieving the optimum effect requires someone with less than very high cholesterol levels to take a smaller daily dose.
    C   Preliminary evidence suggests that the treatment achieves a relatively small reduction in the risk of a heart attack among people with less than very high levels of cholesterol.
    D   Not all the evidence is positive, as people with lower cholesterol levels who take the treatment have been found to develop an increased risk of some cancers.
    E   Originally it was thought that the treatment worked by lowering the cholesterol level, but it is now believed that this effect alone is not enough to account for all the advantages that the treatment provides.

    Answer: [   ]

7. New evidence suggests that the treatment could cut heart attacks by a third.

    A True   B False   C Cannot tell

    Answer: [   ]

8.   Given that the benefits of the treatment are directly proportional to the size of the reduction in cholesterol levels achieved, doctors should look more to the relative drop in cholesterol that may be achieved through the treatment rather than prioritizing patients suffering the very highest levels.

A True   B False   C Cannot tell

Answer: _____

Passage 3

The projection in the latest quarterly inflation report is for growth to pick up to 2.8 per cent. For this forecast to be realized, household spending and domestic consumption would need to increase noticeably from its current lacklustre level. The economy has grown at a rate below its long-term trend for three out of the last four quarters. Wage growth was under control and the high-street and housing markets, while not getting worse, were not getting any better either. Import prices had started to add to inflation after years of deflation, in the wake of the $25 jump in the barrel price of crude. But most economists felt it best to ignore the first-round impact of this rise and wait for any domestic secondary effect – higher prices in the shops – before taking action. That action will almost certainly involve interest rate increases, the effect of which would be to squeeze household spending and knock back inflation. The economy would then have to wait for the stable job markets and increases in incomes and wage growth to diminish the effect of the rate increase over the medium term. Eventually these factors would give rise to domestic growth at or above the long-term trend. In the meantime the risk of either a full-scale consumer recession or a collapse in house prices is very slight.

9.   The main theme of the passage is the question of whether or not oil price inflation must lead to higher interest rates.

A True   B False   C Cannot tell

Answer: _____

10. The author would agree that wage growth and incomes will increase if the job markets remain steady.

    A True   B False   C Cannot tell

    Answer: [   ]

11. The author does not believe that the economy is on target to realize the projection for growth given in the last quarterly inflation report.

    A True   B False   C Cannot tell

    Answer: [   ]

12. Which of the following statements would the author of the passage most likely agree with:

    A   The wider community of economists is split over whether monetary policy should pay heed to the immediate price impact from oil.
    B   Broadly speaking, economists agree that immediate action should be taken against the inflationary effects of the $25 jump in the price of crude.
    C   The wider community of economists rejects the view that the best monetary policy is to take no action over the immediate impacts of the oil price rise.
    D   Most economists are for ignoring any rise in non-oil inflation.
    E   None of the above.

    Answer: [   ]

Passage 4

Road congestion has grown by 37 per cent, and as people switch from private cars to public transport the total distance travelled by rail is expected to increase by 60 per cent. Despite the obvious increase in demand for space on our roads and trains, governments are failing to match forecast growth with investment in either mode of transport. In the 10 worst areas the problems are already chronic, with imme-diate investment needed if sufficient capacity is to be created to cope with future demand. In these areas, new roads and tracks, and longer platforms that can handle longer trains, are already needed to relieve bottlenecks, congestion and severe overcrowding during peak hours. Despite demand, there are no plans to significantly expand road and rail networks, and indeed closures and cuts in funding are on the agenda. The paucity of public investment raises considerable doubts whether those few projects that are currently supported will ever be completed because ministers are refusing to say how much public money they will receive.

13. As road congestion has grown the total distance travelled by rail has increased.

   A True   B False   C Cannot tell

   Answer: [   ]

14. The passage describes the transport infrastructure of northern Europe.

   A True   B False   C Cannot tell

   Answer: [   ]

15. It is hard to arrive at any other conclusion than that travellers face a bleak future of:

   A   Overcrowded networks, slower journey times and higher fares.
   B   Congestion, bottlenecks and overcrowding.
   C   Congestion, overcrowded networks and higher fares.
   D   Overcrowding, congestion and even slower journey times.
   E   Slower journey times and higher fares.

   Answer: [   ]

16. The type of projects that are supported but which may never be completed because of diminutive public investment are:

   A Road projects   B Rail projects
   C Both road and rail projects   D Not specified

   Answer: [   ]

Passage 5

The Agency for Crude Oil estimates that China's imports of crude will increase by 8 per cent year on year, a figure more than twice the predicted rate of growth in global demand. To protect Chinese farmers, the group that has gained least from the economic reforms, and to avoid social unrest, the People's Congress has held the price of diesel at the pumps artificially low. These price controls mean that Chinese state-owned refineries are losing vast sums of money when supplying domestic markets. To offset these losses, the refinery managers must export fuel, and this is the single most important cause of the chronic fuel shortages facing the domestic market of China.

China's energy companies are desperately trying to resolve the issue by securing more suppliers of crude. Their greatest hope lies with Russia, which currently only supplies a small fraction of China's annual consumption. Chinese officials would dearly love a pipeline from the Siberian oilfields. But Russia is anxious to keep control of its export market and is understandably reluctant to provide its neighbour's refineries with oil only to see it sold on to a third party in order to cross-subsidize the artificially low cost of fuel on China's domestic markets.

Perhaps a more viable solution lies with a price increase in the cost of diesel in Chinese domestic markets. This might well mean that the current runaway demand will be curtailed and Chinese refineries will be better able to supply their home markets.

17. Which of the following phases is most appropriate in describing the difficulties China is experiencing over the supply and demand of crude oil for its domestic markets?

A Catastrophe   B Tragedy   C Predicament   D Snag
E Complication

Answer: [   ]

18. Which of the following is mentioned as a solution to fuel shortages:

    A   Securing more suppliers of crude.
    B   A pipeline from the Siberian oilfields.
    C   An end to refineries selling overseas.
    D   An end to the artificially low cost of fuel on China's domestic markets.
    E   Curtailment of the current runaway demand.

    Answer: [   ]

19. Which topic is not touched upon in the passage:

    A Fiscal policy   B International relations   C Fuel exports
    D Retail Price   E Rationing

    Answer: [   ]

20. China is keeping a lid on prices at the pumps to protect the group that has gained least from the economic reforms.

    A True   B False   C Cannot tell

    Answer: [   ]

Passage 6

We may not much like the fact but we are 99.9 per cent identical. This is because 99.9 per cent of our DNA is common to every person, and the Human Genome Project is rightly celebrated for sequencing it. But what of the remaining 0.1 per cent? It is far more significant than one might assume because if it were not for this minute percentage there would be no individual differences. We would be clones. These variations in the human code account for all individual idiosyncrasies. They are responsible for the differences between ethnic and racial groups. Perhaps most interesting of all, they also explain why some of us enjoy good health while others are more susceptible to many common diseases. It is thought that the mapping of the remaining 0.1 per cent of human DNA will hasten the identification of new ways to treat common aliments such as obesity, cancer and heart disease. The work will prove particularly useful in the search for new diagnostic tests, the customizing of treatments to best suit an individual's genetic code, and ultimately the development of new drugs that target the DNA linked to a particular disease. The task of charting the inherited differences in the human genome has fallen to 200 scientists drawn from nine countries across every populated continent. They will screen people drawn from all the major human populations.

21. Sequencing is only mentioned in the passage in relation to the work of the Human Genome Project.

A True   B False   C Cannot tell

Answer: [   ]

22. It can be inferred that the work will:

A   Accelerate the search for genes involved in common diseases.
B   Chart the inherited differences in the human genome.
C   Speed up the development of new treatments.
D   Map the DNA that is shared by every person.
E   Be made freely available on the internet.

Answer: [   ]

23. The issue of preventative therapies is mentioned.

A True   B False   C Cannot tell

Answer: [   ]

24. In reaching the conclusion that some of us enjoy good health
     while others are more susceptible to many common diseases, the
     author relies on the premise:

     A   Humans are 99.9 per cent genetically identical.
     B   The genetic differences between people hold the key to our
         predisposition to many common diseases.
     C   Just 0.1 per cent of the human genetic code accounts for all
         the genetic differences between human beings.
     D   The human genome sequence provides us with a blueprint
         of all the DNA shared by every human being.
     E   The sequencing of the genetic differences allows scientists to
         identify genes that influence common diseases.

Answer: [   ]

Passage 7

We all know that our criminal system is failing, but how many of us
know the extent of the failure? Do you know for example that 9 out of
10 offenders re-offend within two years of completing their
punishment? Our prisons are so overcrowded that programmes of
education and rehabilitation have been abandoned. Offenders rarely
get a prison sentence on the occasion of their first conviction. They are
far more likely to be sentenced to a curfew monitored by an electronic
tag and police surveillance. But by the time they have appeared
before the judge on the third or fourth occasion, all hope that
community-based punishments will work are abandoned and the
persistent offender is sentenced to a period of imprisonment. Of those
who are given a curfew order, many don't even wait for the end of the
period of curfew before re-offending. Large numbers breach their
curfew repeatedly and even remove their electronic tags. Under the
current system even the fear of being caught and punished again is
failing to deter. No wonder crime rates are soaring.

25. Which of the following statements serves as a premise to the author's main claim?

    A   That rehabilitation programmes reduce offending rates.
    B   That today's punishments fail to deter re-offending.
    C   That the objective of punishment is to deter re-offending.
    D   That the frequency of re-offending is increasing.
    E   That crime rates are soaring.

    Answer: [   ]

26. The reason for the abandonment of rehabilitation programmes is that the prisons are so overcrowded prisoners must forgo education and rehabilitation programmes so that staff may concentrate on issues of security.

    A True   B False   C Cannot tell

    Answer: [   ]

27. Which of the following sentences would most likely follow as the next in the passage?

    A   It is abundantly clear that we need to find workable alternative solutions to tackle this very real challenge to society.
    B   Perhaps we need to find other ways to punish those in society who refuse to stop offending.
    C   Persistent offenders need longer sentences that might change their attitude towards rehabilitation programmes and encourage them to reform their criminal behaviour.
    D   It seems beyond the wit of everyone involved to find a workable way of curbing the rate of offending by persistent young offenders.
    E   Recidivism will decline as long as our community and prison based punishments fail to deter the persistent offender.

    Answer: [   ]

28.   The criminal system is slow or unwilling to provide the resources required for rehabilitation provision.

A True   B False   C Cannot tell

Answer: [   ]

Passage 8

We face a pensions crisis because more than half of all working people will rely solely on the state to provide a pension in their old age. These people have paid into a state pension scheme all their working lives. In return they expected to be provided with a state pension on which to live during their old age. Why then the crisis? In the 1960s there was one pensioner for every five workers; this ratio has dropped to one pensioner for every three people in work and is forecast to go as low as one to every two within the next 20 years. The government will simply not be able to provide pensions to the millions of retired people. To make ends meet it is estimated that the government will have to cut the low pension rate by 30 per cent. This means that those who rely solely on the state for a pension may well find themselves retiring to utter poverty. This will directly affect around 12 million people, so it is no wonder people are talking about a crisis. A large slice of the other half of the working population is also at risk of retiring to poverty. These workers have, as well as their state pension, a private scheme to which they contribute and which they intend to use to top up their state pension in retirement. However, most are contributing only a pittance towards these schemes and have funds currently valued at less than $10,000. On their retirement most of these people will find that their private schemes are insufficient to buy them a meaningful second source of income.

29.   In making his case the author relies on the assumption that the government has not been putting aside workers' contributions so that it can meet its future pension commitments.

A True   B False   C Cannot tell

Answer: [   ]

30. The number of people at risk of retiring into poverty is:

   A Less than 12 million   B Exactly 12 million
   C Around 12 million   D More than 12 million

   Answer: [   ]

31. A net influx of migrants would help improve the future pensioner–workers ratio.

   A True   B False   C Cannot tell

   Answer: [   ]

32. Which of the following would most likely follow on as the next sentence in the passage?

   A   The government faces an $800 billion bill for public sector pensions.
   B   They too will not be able to enjoy a decent quality of life in their retirement.
   C   Long-awaited proposals to tackle the looming crisis were rejected out of hand by the government yesterday.
   D   They too eagerly await proposals as to how the crisis might be avoided.
   E   Long-awaited proposals as to how workers can be encouraged to save more for their retirement were announced recently.

   Answer: [   ]

Passage 9

The 1707 Act of Union, the legislation that enshrines the constitutional unification of Scotland and England, passed almost without celebration on its tercentenary. The Scottish National Party (the political party that seeks Scottish withdrawal from the union) is set to take control for the first time of the devolved Scottish Parliament. This once again raises the question of how an independent Scotland might prosper. Much is made of the North Sea oil revenue, which if allocated entirely to Scotland would this year amount to more than £10 billion.

This is by no means a typical year however, as annual oil revenue has averaged nearer £6 billion. Other tax incomes total something in the region of £30 billion annually. Currently, annual expenditure in Scotland is estimated to be approaching £50 billion. To be more definite after so many years of unification is difficult. In any event, a people of 5 million may well be very willing to chance the consequences of independence and capable of achieving a dynamism that overcomes the cost and potential drawbacks of independence.

33.   It is reasonable to infer that the fledgling state of Scotland would:

   A   Face a significant fiscal deficit.
   B   Enjoy an enviable monetary surplus.
   C   Face some hard choices.
   D   Be able to revive its fortunes.

   Answer: [   ]

34.   The author would agree with the assertion that Scotland could afford independence.

   A True   B False   C Cannot tell

   Answer: [   ]

35.   It can be surmised that the state of the economy of an independent Scotland would be:

   A   In no time at all as successful as the Republic of Ireland.
   B   Less dependent on shifts in the world's crude oil markets.
   C   Comparable to that of Sweden.
   D   More dependent on price fluctuations in the price of its crude oil.

   Answer: [   ]

36.   In any split from the United Kingdom of Great Britain, Scotland is unlikely to be allocated the entire proceeds from North Sea oil.

   A True   B False   C Cannot tell

   Answer: [   ]

Passage 10

Since 1997 over 1 million children have seen their family's income rise to the point where they are no longer defined as being in poverty. This has been achieved through an increase in levels of employment and the minimum wage, and increases in the level of state benefits paid to families. Despite these gains, marital break-up, youth unemployment, teenage pregnancy and violent crime committed by young people are all at record high levels. Opponents argue that undeniably greater prosperity has failed to lead to greater social cohesion. They point to the current policies' failure to support the institution of marriage as the principal cause. Fiscal policy, since the abolition of the married couples' allowance and the introduction of the family tax credits, offers no recognition of marriage. Whatever opponents propose, it is likely to include a far greater emphasis on the family unit as one that comprises a married couple both of whom are living with their children. They make it clear that their proposals will equally apply to gay couples caring for children and living in civil partnerships.

37. Youth unemployment is higher than in 1997.

   A True   B False   C Cannot tell

   Answer: [   ]

38. It is reasonable to infer from the passage that an important difference between these two points of view comes down to the definition of the family. The opponents to current policy view it as comprising:

   A   A couple who live with their children.
   B   A married man and woman cohabiting with their children.
   C   A gay couple with parental responsibilities who have made a commitment through a civil partnership.
   D   An unmarried women with children.
   E   None of the above.

   Answer: [   ]

39. The abolition of the married couples allowance occurred in 1997.
     A True   B False   C Cannot tell

                        Answer: [   ]

40. The opponent's family agenda is directed against:
     A   Single mothers.
     B   Absent fathers.
     C   Social cohesion.
     D   Social ills.

                        Answer: [   ]

End of test.

Answers and explanations

Answers and explanations to Chapter 2

Handling data: the essentials

1. East
   All you need to do to answer this type of question is to know the points of the compass and know the directions of clockwise and anticlockwise. Try drawing it out on a piece of paper if you did not get the right answer.
2. West
3. North
4. No
   David could have made his turns in either direction in order to end up facing east.
5. 75p
   £3.00 divided by 4 = 75p.
6. 28
   £21 divided by £3 = 7 packs purchased. Multiply by 4 batteries per pack = 28 batteries.
7. £5.32
   £1.33 multiplied by 4 = £5.32.

8. £18
    £1.50 multiplied by 12 = £18.
9. 16
    48 divided by 3 = 16.
10. £6.24
    Four boxes of eggs are needed. £1.56 multiplied by 4 = £6.24.
11. £5.20
    The price of an egg is £1.56 divided by 6 = 26p. Multiply by 20
    = £5.20.
12. 360 g
    6 multiplied by 60 = 360.
13. 200 g
    Weight of 1 egg is 300 g divided by 6 = 50 g. Multiply by 4 = 200 g.
14. 11
    £132 divided by 12 = 11.
15. 40
    Divide 1,200 (p) by 30 (p) = 40.
16. £8.80
    £16 multiplied by 0.55 = £8.8.
17. 0.25 g
    400 divided by 1,600 = 0.25.
18. 111 g
    There are 37 × 10 = 370 beans. Multiply by the weight of each:
    370 × 0.3 = 111 g.
19. £7.00
    25 multiplied by 28 = 700 pence or £7.00.
20. £66.66
    10.1p multiplied by 660 = 6,666 pence or £66.66.
21. £2.40
    £48 × 5% = £2.4.
22. 12
    100% = 60, 10% = 6 so 20% = 12.
23. 80
    60 minutes divided by 3 = 20 buses per hour. Multiply by 4 = 80
    per shift.
24. 12 minutes
    6 hours consists of 360 minutes, which divided by 30 = 12.
25. 33.3%
    13 is a third of 39 or 33.3%.

26. 7 minutes and 30 seconds
    45 multiplied by 10 = 450 seconds. Divided by 60 to convert to minutes, = 7.5 or 7 minutes 30 seconds.
27. £22.50
    £202.50 divided by 9 = £22.50.
28. £60
    4 multiplied by 30 = 120 divided by 2 = 60.
29. £13.44
    £112 multiplied by 12 = £1344, divided by 100 = £13.44.
30. Yes
    The total VAT cost will be £2,100 which is 17.5% of £12,000.
31. 27
32. Yes
    17.5% of 1,500,000 = 262,500.
33. 1,125 ml
34. 3.25 pm
35. €30.6
36. More
    The vendor would receive about £326,000.
37. 90
    Each litter of 9 multiplied by the 9 piglets = 81 to which you must add the original 9 piglets giving you 90.
38. 3%
    A 1% increase is 5.3 schools so an increase of 16 is equal to just over 3%.

Quantitative reasoning

1. C
   Multiply the price of one dozen by 3.5: 1.2 × 3.5 = 4.2.
2. D
   To calculate the weight of a single parcel, divide the weight of two parcels by two: 0.5/2 = 0.25 kg. Take away the weight of a parcel from the combined weight of a parcel and a letter to get the weight of a letter 0.35 − 0.25 = 0.1. Multiply by two for the weight of two letters: 0.1 × 2 = 0.2.
3. B
   One third of the full price is 33.33%. The remainder is 66.66%, so the discount was 66.66%.

4. F

    One quarter of £24,840 is £6,210. Add that quarter to the year 2000 profit: £24,840 + £6,210 = £31,050.

5. B

    64 – 25% = 48 and 16 – 25% = 12.

6. D

    £277,000 – £67,000 – £21,000 – £103,000 = £86,000.

7. D

    One coach can accommodate 75/3 = 25 passengers. Divide 150 by 25 = 6.

8. A

    Divide the total income by the number of people: £1,134/126 = £9.

9. D

    Sophie spends 1 h 30 mins travelling each way, equals 3 h every day. She works 5 days per week so 3 × 5 = 15.

10. E

    Add up all the overtime hours: 2 + 1.5 + 1 + 2.5 + 3 = 10, then divide by the number of staff: 10/5 = 2.

11. D

    £70 + 5% = £73.50 and £80 – 45% =£ 44. £73.50 + £44 = £117.50 per week.

12. F

    Multiply the number of coins by the fraction of a pound the coin represents: (7 × 1/2 = £3.50) + (18 × 1/5 = £3.60) + (33 × 1/10 = £3.30) + (12 × 1/20 = £0.60) + (15 × 1/50 = £0.30) = £11.30.

13. F

    We can calculate the number of self-employed staff by finding out the percentage 29 members of staff represent. The remaining 24% + 18% = 42%, therefore 29 = 58%. By dividing 29 by 58% we can find out 1%: 29/58 = 0.5 of a member of staff. By multiplying 24% by 0.5 we find out the number of self-employed staff = 12.

14. D

    The ratio of investment between B and A is 1:2.5, therefore the total investment = 3.5. Divide £70,000 by 3.5 = £20,000 = 1 share = B's contribution.

15. C

    Divide the copies per machine per hour by 60 minutes: 180/60 = 3 copies per minute. One photocopier can produce 3 × 25 = 75 copies in 25 minutes. Two photocopiers can produce twice as much = 150 copies.

16. A
    Angela spends 35 hours per week in the office (7 h × 5 days).
    Divide by 7 and multiply by 3: (35/7) * 3 = 15 hours per week
    typing letters.

17. C
    12 m × 18.5 m = 222 sq m × £2.25 = £499.50.

18. F
    £64 as a percentage of £400 is 64/400 × 100 = 16%.

19. D
    Calculate the actual length in cm by multiplying 57.5 by 2,000 =
    115,000 cm. To convert to metres, divide by 100: 115,000/100
    = 1,150 m.

20. C
    There are 3.5 times more female than male workers. 4 × 3.5 = 14.

21. D
    The total amount needed for the trip is €400 × 4 days = €1,600.
    To convert to sterling, divide by the exchange rate: 1,600/1.6 =
    £1,000.

22. A
    John and Sarah together earn £46,700 (18,700 + 28,000). Mark
    earns 53% of this amount (47% less than John and Sarah). 1%
    = £467; 53% = £24,751.

23. B
    2000: £1,250 × 110% = £1,375. 2001: £1,375 × 110% =
    £1,512.50.

24. A
    Divide the total number of employees by the sum of the ratio:
    370/10 = 37. Multiply by the 7 old: = 259.

25. C
    The annual target is 150 sales × 4 quarters = 600. Average 137
    per quarter × 3 quarters = 411. 600 – 411 = 189.

26. A
    The £15,400 equals 100% minus 23% of the secretary's income
    = 77%. Her full income is 15,400/77*100 = £20,000.

27. E
    First we need to find out how many people Company A
    employs. If Company C employs 25% fewer than A, then 120 =
    75%; 120/75 = 1.6 × 100 = 160. Therefore, Company A
    employs 160 people. Ratio A to B is 2:1 so Company B employs
    160/2 = 80 people.

28.   B
      The office area is 11 m × 12.5 m = 137.5 sq m. Deduct the area
      underneath the cabinet: 125 cm × 80 cm = 10,000 sq cm which
      converts to 1 sq m, so the area to be carpeted is 136.5 sq m. Four
      tiles 50 cm by 50 cm are required to carpet each sq m, so the
      total needed is 136.5 × 4 = 546.
29.   E
      £3,700 − 35% = £2,405. The amount of this proportion spent
      is 3/12 on the speaker and 8/12 on the transport = 11/12, so
      1/12 is left for refreshments: 2,405/12 = £200.4167, which
      rounds to £200.

Data interpretation

Table 2.1
1.   D
     Can clearly be seen from table.
2.   B
     Can clearly be seen from table.
3.   D
     4.5 New Commonwealth + 3.1 Rest of the World = 7.6 (thousand).
4.   C
     3.9 (thousand) in 2000 − 3.7 (thousand) in 1985 = 0.2 (thousand)
     = 200.
5.   B
     16/40 = 40%.

Table 2.2
6.   B
     The ferry leaves Pier Head on the hour and returns 50 minutes
     later.
7.   B
     Can clearly be seen from table.
8.   E
     Between 3.50 pm and 4.15 pm.
9.   D
     50 × £2.20 = £110.00.

10. E

   A 15 minute delay on the last four journeys would result in an hour's delay overall, so the finish time is 6.15 pm + 1 hour = 7.15 pm.

Table 2.3

11. D

   Can clearly be seen from table.

12. B

   Can easily be calculated from table.

13. D

   475 less 325.

14. C

   200°C * 105% = 210°C.

Figure 2.1

15. A

   Can clearly be seen from table: PURE ORANGE JUICEX1LTR.

16. D

   2 multisave items: £1.79 + £1.99 = £3.78.

17. E

   Although the total items indicated by 'g' add up to £8.27, there is a multisave of £1.79 on S SATSUMA LARGE; thus £8.27 − £1.79 = £6.48.

18. C

   £302.60 * 10% = £30.26.

Table 2.4

19. C

   23 days entitlement − 1 taken last year − 11 taken in the current year = 11.

20. D

   Hasan receives 26 days, which equals a basic 23 days for the first two years' service plus 3 more days. This is 1 day per year (half a day per half year) so he has been with the company for 3 plus 2 years = 5 years in total.

21. C

   23 days annual entitlement − 1.5 days taken last year − 8 days taken in the current year = 13.5 days. £300/5 = £60 × 13.5 = £810.

22.   E
S. Brown has 23 less 12 days' holiday left (1 taken last year, 11 taken in the current year) = 11 days. If he takes these 11, he needs 4 more days of unpaid leave.

Table 2.5

23.   C
31 (units sold) × £49 (price per package) = £1,519 sales income. 3% commission = £45.57.

24.   A
24 + 31 + 28 + 21 + 26 + 26 = 156/6= 26.

25.   E
The commission for the first 25 units is calculated at 3% and equals £36.75. The commission for the three units achieved over the target is calculated at 5% and equals £7.35. This gives a total of £44.10.

26.   E
Four out of 6 employees reached the target.

Table 2.6

27.   C
The most profitable product is identified by subtracting the total cost from the sales price.

28.   D
Reducing the manufacturing cost of £2 by 50% will add £1 to the sales revenue for each unit sold. So the sales revenue is the existing £37,625 plus £21,500 = £59,125.

29.   B
£7.99 – £5.37 = £2.62 (revenue per unit) × 11,750 (number of units) = £30,785.

30.   A
23% of £743,578.00 = £171,022.94 tax paid. £743,578.00 – £171,022.94 = £572,555.06 net profit.

Table 2.7

31.   A
(0 + 10 + 21.5 + 4)/4 = 8.9 approx.

32.   B
3.5 – (–1) = 4.5°C.

33. C
34. F
     Cumulative temperature in 2000: (1.5 + 15.5 + 23 + 2) = 42.
     Final quarter 2001 is 42 – 2 – 14.5 – 25= 0.5.

Word swap

1. movement/tone
2. work/result
3. artificial/natural
4. some/and
5. remain/recess
6. most/each
7. to/is
8. style/hunger
9. over/now
10. by/of
11. eat/respect
12. kill/catch
13. rake/forget
14. numerous/bitter
15. adaptable/Roman
16. inserted/impervious
17. idyllic/irritating
18. known/health
19. about/without

Missing words

1. B, effect effect
2. C, dependent dependant
3. B, accepted licence
4. B, conscience conscious
5. A, threw rear
6. B, hew hue
7. C, principle principal
8. A, courtesy curtsy
9. B, dispensary disciplinary
10. C, hoard horde

11.   C, flowers flour
12.   D, piece pierce
13.   B, inform infirm
14.   B, practice practise
15.   A, stationary stationery
16.   D, receipt recipe
17.   D, exercises immediately
18.   B, minor operate
19.   A, boys boys'
20.   B, it's its
21.   B, plumb straight

Correct sentences

1.   a) If you're looking for an evening out this month, there are big offers on musicals and pop concerts.
2.   b) The consumer is protected from exploitation by a given seller by the existence of other sellers from whom he can buy.
3.   c) All mammals produce eggs within which their young develop.
4.   a) There are maps and travel books available for most of England's towns and cities.
5.   c) Further information will be given to you when you visit the head office.
6.   a) She married again, which surprised everybody who knew her.
7.   b) There is a wide selection of gifts available, all of which can be ordered by post or online.
8.   a) At that moment, I wished I had gone to the same university as John.
9.   c) When I go to university I will have no time for reading novels.
10. b) The coach was expecting great things of the team this season.
11. a) Whenever a new book comes out she is the first to buy a copy.
12. b) There is the promise of a more secure future for those who save on a regular basis.
13. c) If the customer should return the goods, you must ensure you check them before giving a refund.
14. b) There are places where that kind of behaviour is unacceptable.
15. a) This borough is very good about providing bins for recycling metal, plastic, glass and paper.
16. c) One of the most important notes on the piano is Middle C.

17. b) Once Simon gets angry it takes a long while for him to calm down.
18. a) We pitched our tent on the bank of the river Stour, near where it joins the Avon.
19. c) They were walking along the beach all day yesterday and they will be walking along the cliff all day tomorrow.
20. a) It was Galileo who discovered that Jupiter has moons.

Following procedures

1. B
2. E
3. E
4. D
5. E, G, H
6. D
7. G, H
8. F
9. E, F, I
10. D

Speed and accuracy

1. B, 3 pairs
2. E, None
3. C, 2 pairs
4. E, None
5. C, 2 pairs
6. E, None
7. C, 2 pairs
8. D, 1 pair
9. B, 3 pairs
10. C, 2 pairs
11. E, None
12. C, 2 pairs
13. B, 3 pairs
14. A, all 4
15. A, all 4
16. A, all 4
17. B, 3 pairs
18. B, 3 pairs
19. C, 2 pairs
20. C, 2 pairs
21. D, 1 pair
22. D, 1 pair
23. D, 1 pair

Answers and explanations to Chapter 3

Practice test 1: quantitative reasoning

1. F
    $(7 \times 27) + (4 \times 19) = 265p = £2.65.$
2. D
    $14.45 + 27 m = 15.12$

3. F
    End of year 1: 1,000.00 × 105% = £1,050.00. End of year 2:
    1,050.00 × 105% = £1,102.50. End of year 3: 1,102.50 × 105%
    = £1,157.63.
4. C
    End of year 1: 800 – 40% = £480. End of year 2: 480 – 25% =
    £360. End of year 3: 360 – 25% = £270.
5. F
    30 wpm × 30 min = 900 words.
6. E
    1.25 × 4 = 5.
7. D
    (2 × 1.75) + (5 × 1.15) = 9.25 × 1.175% = £10.87.
8. B
    18,900/9 = 2,100. 2,100 × 3 = 6,300.
9. D
    1 kg/5 = 200 g. £3.50/5 = £0.70.
10. A
    The return journey takes 1.5 h. The meeting takes another 1.5 h.
    The total time spent away from the office is 3 h.
11. D
    20% = 1 in 5, so 10 members of staff must join to qualify for two
    free memberships.
12. C
    The price of two items = 100%. If one item is free 50% is saved.
13. C
    3.4/4.3 = 0.79 × 2.3 = £1.82.
14. B
    The question requires you to find the time difference between
    38/47 of an hour and 29/38 of an hour. These fractions can be
    treated as convenient equivalents to 4/5 and 3/4 of an hour = 48
    and 45 minutes. Hence, 3 minutes difference.
15. F
    If £24 is 3%, then 1% is 24/3 = £8, and 100% = £800.
16. D
    The new price is £10 – 25% = £7.50. £1,000/£7.50 = 133.33.
    The sales should increase by 33.3%.

17. E
The ratio of staple boxes can be expressed as 1 : 1.5 : 2.25 : 3.375, which sums to 8.125. 1,000 g/8.13 = 123 × 3.375 = 415.125 g.

18. C
3.5% of 1,000 = £35. To obtain £35 commission B must sell 35/.03 goods, which is £116.67 worth.

19. E
The time difference between Dubai and New York is 10 hours. It is 10 hours earlier in Dubai so the conference will start at 04.30 am on 11 January.

20. F
The ratio is 2:7:1 which can also be expressed as = 1:3.5:0.5.

21. D
100/20 = 5 × 3 = 15%.

22. F
7.99 × 0.305 = £2.44.

23. B
225/0.45 = 500.

24. C
In 30 mins it will travel 17.5 miles, which divided by 0.621 equals 28 km approx.

25. C
£12/25 = £0.48 per minute. £0.48 × 45 = £21.60.

26. E
If 1 ft = 0.305 m, 1 sq ft = (0.305 × 0.305) sq m = 0.093 sq m. Price per sq m: £6.25/0.093 = £67.20. Price for 5 sq m = £67.20 × 5 = £336.

27. D
{35 mph + (35/2)}/2 = 52.5/2 = 26.25.

28. B
(5,000 + 1,000) × 2 = 12,000. (12,000 + 1,000) × 2 = £26,000.

29. F
1.83 m = (1.83/0.305) = 6 ft. 12 files per ft, so 6 × 12 = 72 files can be stored.

30. B
Distance/time 56 miles/70 min = 0.8 miles per minute.0.8 miles per minute × 60 min = 48 mph.

Practice test 2: data interpretation

Table 3.1

1. B
    Readily seen from table.
2. D
    64 + 39 + 95 + 40 + 17 + 14 = 269.
3. D
    33/ 200 × 100 = 16.5%.
4. C
    42/300 × 100 = 14%, the lowest percentage.

Table 3.2

5. E
    280 rand/selling price 3.18 = £88.05.
6. B
    1,750.00 × 2.99– 4.5% = 4,997.03.
7. E
    4,997.03/2.79 = 1,791.05 – 4.5% = 1,710.45.
8. A
    (1.55 +1.66)/2=1.605 average rate. €0.5/1.605 = £0.31.

Table 3.3

9. D
    1/6 = 16.66%.
10. F
    £1 per week × 26.5 = £26.50.
11. C
    £23.45 – £20 + £800 – £95 = £708.45.
12. A
    – £250 + £360 – £25 = £85.

Table 3.4

13. C
    A package to Aberdeen = £1.66 + £0.85 = £2.51. A letter to
    France = £0.37.
14. A
    0.96 kg = 960 g = 500 g + 460 g. 500 (£1.66) + 250 (£0.85) +
    210 (£0.85) = £3.36.

15. F

100 g to Europe = £0.99 + 350 g to UK = £1.30 = £2.29.

16. E

Separately: £1.05 + £1.79 = £2.84. Together: £2.16 + £1.25 = £3.41. Difference: £0.57.

Table 3.5

17. B

If there were 9.2 deaths per 1,000, then there were 9,200 deaths per million. Since there are 83 million people in Germany = 9,200 × 83 = 763,600.

18. B

Total births – total deaths = 3 per thousand = 3,000 deaths per million = 3,000 × 60 = 180,000.

19. C

End of 2001 = 60,180,000 total population. End of 2002 = 60,180,000 × 100. 3% = 60,360,540.

20. E

Total births – total deaths per year.

Table 3.6

21. F

Arable land, permanent pasture and woodland = 33%.
Therefore 67% of land = 545,630 × 67% = 365,572 sq km.

22. C

1km = 0.625 miles. 1 sq km = 0.39 sq m. 41,526 × 0.39 = 16,195.14.

23. F

7,643/41,526 = 18.4%.

24. F

30% of 504,782.

Practice test 3: correct sentences

1.   b) If she had only listened to me, this would never have happened.
2.   c) There are just three things you need to know about Jack.
3.   b) If I were you I'd see a doctor.
4.   a) It looks like everyone has gone to the cinema.
5.   b) Either Jane or her sister is bringing the dessert.

6. c) If I hadn't had my seatbelt on I would be dead.
7. b) From Thursday you cannot have either the blue or the black pens.
8. a) I have been informed that neither Mandy nor Helen will be able to be there on Saturday.
9. b) Owning a dog is very different from owning a cat.
10. None of these.
11. c) If you were to go fishing at night you might find that you caught more fish than during the day.
12. a) Although the house and barn are on the same property, they will be sold separately.
13. d) None of these.
14. b) The Managing Director wanted you and me to attend the meeting.
15. b) Each night before I go to bed I make myself a cup of cocoa.
16. a) Carol thought it an honour to receive an MBE.
17. c) It looks as if it is going to rain.
18. b) Every one of the new computers in the main office has been virus checked.
19. c) It is equally as important to check your credit card statement as it is your bank statement.
20. c) Mike always seems to do it that way.

Practice test 4: following procedures

Situation 1
1. E (Mr D. Fryer)
    The rules state that only the regional director can approve purchases from a non-approved supplier, and this supplier is not on the approved list.
2. B (Tom Mosby)
    Area managers can approve purchases for their area only from approved suppliers to a maximum of £100,000.
3. A and B (Diana Jordon and Alex Matthews)
    Administrative officers can approve expenditure in their area with approved suppliers to a maximum of 1,000.
4. E
    Only Maria Key is not allowed to approve this purchase.

5. B

The rules state that any expenditure over £100,000 must be approved by the appropriate area manager and the regional director.

Situation 2

6. D

The terms state that a 20% fee is charged up to £19,999 and 25% on salaries over £20,000. but the percentage charged on salaries of £20,000 is not given.

7. B

It is stated in the terms that a 50% rebate applies if the employee leaves after 8 weeks but before 12 weeks of employment.

8. F

You can calculate the apportioned pro-rata amount due as 50% of the annual salary = $16,000 \div 2 = £8,000$ plus the £2,000 for the benefit of the car, and the 15% tax.

Situation 3

9. C and E

The procedures state that a final reminder is issued on the 15th working day and that an invoice becomes overdue at that point. In the text prior to the procedures, it is stated that at the weekly meeting with Mr Jones accounts with overdue invoices should be reviewed.

10. B and D

It is stated in the situation that Mrs Smith and her assistant Tina hold this responsibility.

11. D

The passage states that the pair decide whether or not to refer an account to the company's firm of solicitors for advice as to whether there is a case for issuing legal proceedings. This is not the same as the options given in the suggested answers.

Situation 4

12. C

Note that the questions ask which of the suggested answers would LEAST support the applicant's case. C would least support the case because Rule 5 makes it clear that under these circumstances the tribunal would find the case to have failed.

13.   A
      In these circumstances you would expect the tribunal to apply
      Rule 4 and ask the employer to explain the unequal treatment.
14.   B
      Assuming that the tribunal accepted the employer's explanation,
      then according to Rule 4 the application would fail despite the
      fact that there was evidence of different treatment.

Situation 5

15.   C
      This is stated in rule 3.
16.   C
      While the maximum charge shown is 1.25%, this does not mean
      that there is a rule capping any charge above this amount.
17.   B
      He has been undercharged not overcharged; the fee should have
      been charged at 1/365th of 1.25% of his fund.

Practice test 5: speed and accuracy

1.	B, 2 pairs	18.	A, 1 pair	35.	B, 2 pairs
2.	C, 3 pairs	19.	E, None	36.	A, 1 pair
3.	C, 3 pairs	20.	C, 3 pairs	37.	A, 1 pair
4.	E, None	21.	E, None	38.	D, 4 pairs
5.	A, 1 pair	22.	A, 1 pair	39.	E, None
6.	D, 4 pairs	23.	D, 4 pairs	40.	E, None
7.	C, 3 pairs	24.	A, 1 pair	41.	C, 3 pairs
8.	A, 1 pair	25.	D, 4 pairs	42.	B, 2 pairs
9.	E, None	26.	A, 1 pair	43.	D, 4 pairs
10.	E, None	27.	B, 2 pairs	44.	D, 4 pairs
11.	C, 3 pairs	28.	A, 1 pair	45.	E, None
12.	E, None	29.	E, None	46.	E, None
13.	A, 1 pair	30.	A, 1 pair	47.	A, 1 pair
14.	B, 2 pairs	31.	B, 2 pairs	48.	C, 3 pairs
15.	A, 1 pair	32.	D, 4 pairs	49.	B, 2 pairs
16.	D, 4 pairs	33.	B, 2 pairs	50.	E, none
17.	B, 2 pairs	34.	A, 1 pair		

Answers and explanations to Chapter 4

Warm-up questions for the Data interpretation test

Figure 4.1

1. A

   Brian will not be 45 until his birthday the next day.

2. D

   The difference between 1985 and 1955, both being born on the same day.

3. D

   The only time when Brian and James were both aged 4 years is between 17.01.1964 (James's 4th birthday) and 01.02.1964 (the eve of Brian's 5th birthday).

4. B

   If the difference is equal to 25%, then £15.00 must be 75%. Therefore £15.00/3 = 25% = £5.00.

Table 4.1

5. E

   Air, commodity and ship brokers have the lowest percentage increase at 22.0%.

6. E

   For 2001: total earnings = £1,000,685, average earnings = £1,000,685/20 = £50,034.25. For 1991: total earnings = £617,395, average earnings = £617,395/20 = £30,869.75. Therefore 2001 average − 1991 average = £50,034.25 − £30,869.75 = £19,164.50.

7. D

   To be ranked first, air traffic planners and controllers must earn at least £110,342 in 2001 (£1 more than general managers). This would be an increase from their 1991 earnings of (£110,342 − £27,476)/£27,476 * 100 = 301.6%.

8. C

   An increase of 166.3% would produce a salary of £47,007, placing professional athletes 8th, above industrial underwriters and claims assessors, but below doctors.

Table 4.2

9.   D

Growth in earnings increased by £11.40 between 1989 and 1990, higher than any other year.

10.   E

£353.40 – £227.60 = £125.80.

11.   A

£353.40 – £259.70 = £93.70/£259.70 * 100 = 36.1%.

12.   B

Average non-manual men's wages (£285.46) – average manual men's wages (£205.23) = £80.23.

Table 4.3

13.   C

Addition of the 1991 figures for Higher, Further and Adult Education (£3,734 million) + Polytechnics and Colleges Funding Council (£993 million) = £4,727 million.

14.   F

8,287 – 5,523 = 2,764/5,523 * 100 = 50.0%.

15.   E

Total expenditure (£34,041 million) = 5.1% of GDP. Therefore (£34,041/5.1) * 100 = £667,471 million.

16.   B

VAT amount (£2,705)/Sub-total of expenditure before VAT (£21,913 + £2, 678) = £24,591 = 11.0%.

Table 4.4

17.   D

The range between lowest low water (1.0 m) and highest high water (9.3 m).

18.   A

Average low water height throughout the week for mornings is 1.8 m; for afternoons it is 1.9 m.

19.   F

Care must be taken when calculating time. The length of sunlight must be calculated as part of the 60-minute clock. Therefore, if sunset was at 18:59 (two minutes earlier than recorded) the daylight hours would be: 18:59 – 05:23 = 13 h 36 m, plus the two minutes to 1901 = 13 h 38 m.

20. E
A high tide 35 minutes before Liverpool would bring the Liverpool high tide in the afternoon into the morning at Southport; ie 12:16 − 35 = 11:41.

Table 4.5

21. C
To find the median simply put the values in size order, the median value is the middle one.

22. E
Find the range by subtracting the lowest number from the highest, but if the lowest number is a negative then remember − − = + so add the negative number to the highest to find the distance between the two values.

23. A
There is nothing approximate about the answer. The suggestion that the answer may only be a close representation was included so as to undermine you. Unfair? Not really: you should show decisiveness and clarity of mind when the data are confused or even misleading. Find the 2005 value then find the increase. The value has increased 1.6% so 101.6% = 406,400, 1% = 406,400/101.6 = 4,000, the investment in 2005 = 100 × 4,000 = 400,000, the increase was $6,400.

24. C
This is one for the calculator. You should be able to see that the answer is either UK or US shares and so need only undertake these calculations. It is wrong to simply work out the percentage change of the 2006 value, as this is the value after the increase. You must first find the value before the increase. In the case of US shares 109.8% = 1,976,400, so the sum at the start of 2006 = 1,800,000 and the sum made was $176,400, while the sum made on UK shares was $175,200.

25. F
The value of the investment at the end of 2006 is £700,000, and the formula for the compound interest earned is F. Formula D would provide the final value of the fund.

The pie chart and table 4.6

26. B

    If you answered C you shared a common misunderstanding that is worth getting right without wasting time on working it through. The company may triple the net profit but it will increase by 200% (because you have to subtract the percentage that you started with). For instance, $0.35 \times 3 = 1.05$, $0.35 \times 200\% = 0.7$ (plus the original 0.35) = 1.05.

27. E

    First calculate the net profit per unit sold, then calculate the net profit for 'Want to Be'. 9.99 – retails commission and all costs of sales = $0.35 per unit × 2 million = $700,000.

28. B

    First calculate the odds for buying a unit manufactured by Competitor: 30% = 0.3, then multiply (the events should be treated as independent) by the probability of it being faulty = $0.3 \times 0.1 = 0.03$.

29. B

    First calculate the range of data – the sales figures for the three companies – and then calculate the mean. Want to Be's 2 m sales = 10% of the market, so the range is 2 m + 6 m + 12 m = 20 m ÷ 3 = 6.6 (to one decimal point).

30. D

    The business model is dated 2006 so in 2002 it had been in use for 4 years. $9.99/(1.05)4 = 9.99 \div 1.05 = 9.514 \div 1.05 = 9.061 \div 1.05 = 8.629 \div 1.05 = 8.218 = \$8.22$

Warm-up questions for the Verbal Test

Passage 1

1. A

    The blue line is described as running north–south and the red line runs east–west so the angle at the point of intersection must be 90 degrees.

2. A

    It is clear from the text that the blue line runs north–south and the red line east–west. It is also said that the green line intersects the red line east of the blue line and the grey line intersects the blue line south of the red line. This means that the grey line would intersect the red line west of the green line.

3. B

    As the blue line runs north–south the intersections of the yellow
    and green line with the blue line will take place at the same
    east–west position.

4. C

    There is no information contained within the text to indicate the
    starting or end positions of the lines.

Passage 2

5. B

    It is clear from the text that the eurozone rate is expected to
    remain unchanged.

6. A

    It is stated that the yen's recent strength is not sustainable.

7. C

    It is unclear from the passage whether or not the two currencies
    are at present aligned or will continue to be.

Passage 3

8. A

    As Team 4 has won more games than Team 1 and has not lost
    any games, Team 4 must have more points than Team 1 as they
    have played the same number of games.

9. B

    Team 3 has seven more points than Team 2 and Team 6 has four
    more points than Team 2. This means that Team 3 has three
    more points than Team 6.

10. C

    Although it can be proved from the passage that Team 2 will
    have fewer points than any other of the teams listed, we do not
    know how many teams there are in the league. This means that
    it is possible there are other teams in the league and that they
    may have fewer points than Team 2.

Passage 4

11. C

    The passage makes no comment on this issue.

12. A

    This can clearly be seen from the passage.

13. B

The principal point concerns the enhancement of a manager's decisions by the incorporation of tests in the overall decision-making process.

Passage 5

14. A

This answer is clearly correct from the passage.

15. A

Because it rains consecutively on a Friday/Saturday there are only three days which follow rain, but on which it does not rain. We also know that two of these days must be Sundays. As there are two occasions on which the sky is clear all day after the rain, at least one of these must be a Sunday.

16. C

This is only true if it rains on the first Wednesday and the first Friday. As the passage does not identify which days it rains on each week, we cannot confirm that this is true.

Passage 6

17. B

You also need to meet the earnings requirement.

18. A

17.5% of £30,000 = £5,250.

19. A

The passage states that all contributions qualify for tax relief at the highest rate paid by the saver.

Passage 7

20. A

It is stated that the bedrooms are on the second floor and the kitchen family room is on the third.

21. C

The size of the reception room is not given.

22. A

While the text does not state which floor the reception room is on, it can be deduced that it is on the first because it is the only floor not described.

Passage 8

23. B
A keyboard can be used to input to a command interface but it is not a command interface.

24. A
It is clear from the text that application software consists of user-related programmes.

25. A
The passage states that the user interface is such a means of communication and it is also described as the human–computer interface.

Passage 9

26. A
The passage clearly states that the velocity and displacement of straight-line motion can be attributed negative values.

27. C
The rules of dynamics are not covered in the passage.

28. B
The statement is true with respect to the forces that act on the particle but is false overall because the passage makes clear that the discipline is not limited to the study of particle motion in straight lines.

Passage 10

29. A
Australia is in the southern hemisphere so depressions would generate winds in the opposite direction to the anticlockwise winds of a northern hemisphere depression.

30. A
The passage states that winds in depressions are revolving. As a depression passes the town therefore, it would experience winds in opposite directions on either side of the depression. This would be the experience in either hemisphere.

31. B
In the northern hemisphere it would be your left ear; in the southern hemisphere it would be your right.

Passage 11

32. B

The insurance broker is on the same side of the road as the off-licence while the pharmacist is on the same side as the newsagent. It is clear, therefore, that they are not on the same side of the road, as the newsagent is described as directly opposite the off-licence.

33. A

The bus stop is across the road from the optician, which in turn is across the road from the pharmacist. This means that the bus stop and the pharmacist are on the same side of the road.

34. B

There is a two-shop gap between the post office and off-licence, and this gap is in part taken up by either the clothes shop or butcher. In either event this leaves insufficient space for the optician and insurance broker. This means that the optician cannot be next to the butcher.

Passage 12

35. C

The work would end in the right-hand corner only if the worker started each line of boards in the left-hand corner, but the instructions only state that the first line is started in this way.

36. A

The end board will be cut to fit the space that remains, and is likely to result in a longer or shorter leftover piece. This is to be used to start the next row so long as the difference in lengths is greater than 50 cm.

37. A

As the board is described as having a long and short side, you can deduce that the short end of the board can be called its end.

Passage 13

38. B

The passage states that it takes Steve less time than James to get to the meeting and that it takes James 9 minutes, so the statement must be false.

39. A

As it takes James longer to get to the meeting than Steve or Helen, and he sets off after Helen, he must arrive after she does.

40.   C
      Although Richard has to travel further we have no indication of
      how long his journey will take and so whether he would need to
      set off first in order to arrive first.

Answers and explanations for Chapter 5

Practice test 1: data interpretation

Situation 1
1.   C
     All the other periods have at least one subsidized session during
     the month.
2.   B
     Addison, Baldock, Clark, Edwards, Gordon, Humphreys,
     Isaacs, Jordan, Lloyd, Milton, Newton and Orwell all pay full
     rate: 12 @ £5.00 = £60.00.
     Dickinson, Fitch and Keith all have subsidized sessions: 3 @
     £2.50 = £7.50.
     Humphreys has a solo extra lesson: 1 @ £6.00 = £6.00.
     Clark and Gordon share an extra lesson: 2 @ £3.50 = £7.00.
     Therefore: £60.00 + £7.50 + £6.00 + £7.00 = £80.50.
3.   D
     Starting at 13.00: No change, remains Milton (M).
     13.30: revised to Orwell (O).
     14.00: No change, remains Lloyd (L).
     14.30: revised to Edwards (E).
     15.00 and 15.30 cancelled.
4.   C
     £212.00/£4.00 = 53 tickets sold by 15 people = 3.5 tickets per
     person.

Situation 2
5.   B
     Old rates: £180 (early July) + £230 (late July) = £410
     minus new rates: £140 (early July) + £180 (late July) = £320.
     Therefore the saving is £410 – £320 = £90.

6. A

£65.00 (new tax) – £42.00 (old Tax) = £23.00 × 6,731 (fares sold)
= £154,813.

7. D

Old price: £200 (July) + £250 (August)) = £450.

New price: £150 (July) + (200 – 25% = £150) (saving in August)
= £300.

Saving: £450 – £300 = £150.

8. C

Although the increase in price for Tenerife is the largest (£100),
it is not the greatest percentage increase.

Lanzarote: new fare £275 (August) – £180 (July) = £95/£180 *
100 = 52.78%.

Tenerife: new fare £300 (August) – £200 (July) = £100/£200 *
100 = 50.00%.

Situation 3

9. D

£356.16 * 48 months = £17,095.68.

10. C

Repayment of £154.21 * 60 months = £9,252.60 + £598.80
difference = £9,851.40.

11. B

24 months at £454.98 will cost Mr Patel £10,919.52; all the
others will cost him more overall.

12. F

Without the disclosure of the variable administration fee this
figure cannot be calculated.

Situation4

13. D

Other industries. Three sets of data increase (road transport, other
industries and residential); from the graph you can estimate that
other industries saw the largest relative (percentage) increase, from
27 to 29 million tonnes.

14. D

The levels of emission are 63:27, which simplifies to 7:3.

15.   C
      You are asked to calculate what year emissions were approxi-
      mately 20 million tonnes if they grew 10% a year prior to 1993.
      As with most questions there are a number of ways to approach
      this question. One is to start with 20 and calculate a 110%
      increase to establish a four-year total of 29.282. 1993 – 4 = 1989.

16.   D
      50% 2007 levels of emissions from road and residential (total
      54.82 million tonnes ÷ 2) = 27.41, total 2007 emissions = 100%
      = 153.46, – 27.41 = 126.05. Estimate the percentage equivalent
      of the fraction 126.05/153.46 e.g. = 125/150 = 5/6 = 83%, a
      reduction of 17%, so answer is between 15 and 20%.

Situation 5

17.   E
      The rate has decreased; to express that decrease as a percentage
      0.021 ÷ 100 = 0.00021, 0.01995 ÷ 0.00021 = 95; therefore
      change = –5%.

18.   A
      You must calculate a 4% increase on 0.055, 0.055 × 104% =
      0.0572, so answer A.

19.   C
      Today's rate has decreased by 6% on yesterday; you must find
      94% of 0.00084. 0.00084 × 94% = 0.0007896, answer C.

20.   D
      In an export-dependent economy a strengthening of the currency
      would help hold inflation down, not fuel it. Street protests would
      not normally strengthen a currency, and outflows of money
      would normally be expected to weaken a currency.

Practice test 2: verbal test

Passage 1

1.   B
      The passage does not conclude that the internet has made
      policing of coursework impossible.

2.   A

It is correct to describe between 20 and 60% as significant. You might describe the extent of plagiarism or cheating as a scandal but not the percentage of marks that are achieved through home-completed assignments.

3.   D

In the passage reference is made to a review and, at one point, the view of candidates is provided in quotation marks. This is sufficient for us to conclude that the passage relies on the findings of an investigative study. Comparative assertions are simply qualified statements.

4.   B

The passage comments on examinations in which home-completed assignments contribute to the grade awarded. It is not reasonable therefore to draw conclusions about vocational qualifications which may or may not include home-completed assignments that contribute to grades.

Passage 2

5.   B

The passage states that every person at risk can gain considerable benefits from the treatment and the statement is false because it says *not* every person.

6.   C

The claim is about the risk of a vascular event and not about the risk of cancer. So the correct answer must weaken the link between a lower risk of a heart attack resulting from the treatment in people with less than the highest levels of cholesterol. Only C does this by suggesting that the reduced risk is relatively small, rather than not much lower as claimed in the question.

7.   B

Reference to a third relates to the group most at risk of an attack. It is stated in the passage that new evidence suggests that patients with less than very high levels of cholesterol will also experience a significant drop in their cholesterol levels and a consequent lower risk of a vascular event.

8.   A

The benefits are directly proportional to the size of reduction in cholesterol levels, and therefore it can be inferred that when deciding who should benefit doctors should consider the size of drop in cholesterol that can be achieved, rather than giving the treatment to those with the highest initial levels.

Passage 3

9.   B

The main theme of the passage is the issue of domestic growth, and the issue of interest rate increases resulting from higher oil prices is examined in the context of what effect this might have on growth.

10.   A

The author refers to the stable job market and (consequent) increases in income and wages as the factors that will give rise to domestic growth on or above the long-term trend.

11.   A

The passage states that for the forecast to be realized household spending and domestic consumption would need to increase noticeably.

12.   E

The passage states that most economists agree with the monetary policy of ignoring the first-round impact of this rise in the price of oil and waiting for any domestic second effect – higher prices in the shops – before taking action. Therefore the author would not agree with any of the suggested answers.

Passage 4

13.   B

The answer is false because it is stated in the passage that an increase in train journey miles is forecast.

14.   C

The passage refers to governments rather than any particular government, which suggests that the area discussed includes more than one country, but no indication is given of which countries the passage relates to.

15.   B

The passage does not mention journey times or higher fares.

16.   D

The passage states: 'the paucity of public investment raises considerable doubts that those few projects that are currently supported will ever be completed because ministers are refusing to say how much public money they will receive.' But which type of projects are supported is not detailed.

Passage 5

17.   C

The passage supports a description of the challenge as a predicament because whatever action is taken will have negative consequences.

18.   D

Only D is mentioned explicitly as a solution to fuel shortages; the others are factors or alternatives which may not eventuate.

19.   E

Fiscal policy concerns the way governments spend and tax in order to achieve goals; this topic is covered in the passage in terms of the Chinese policy of keeping the price of oil products artificially low. International relations between Russia and China are touched upon in the passage, as are the topics of fuel exports and retail price of diesel at the pump. But rationing is not discussed.

20.   True

This is explicitly stated in the passage.

Passage 6

21.   A

A careful read of the passage show that sequencing is indeed only mentioned in the passage in relation to the work of the Human Genome Project.

22.   A

It is stated that the mapping of human genetic differences will hasten the identification of new ways to treat common aliments. It can be inferred that this will be possible because the map will accelerate the search for genes involved in common diseases. B and C are explicitly stated in the passage.

23.   B

New treatments and diagnostic tests are mentioned in the passage, but preventative therapies are not touched upon.

24. **B**

It is the claim that some of our genetic differences explain our propensity for particular diseases that supports the conclusion that some of us enjoy good health while others are more susceptible to many common diseases.

Passage 7

25. **C**

The main claim of the passage is that our criminal system is failing to prevent re-offending. This claim is premised on the assumption that the prevention of re-offending is the principal objective of the criminal system.

26. **B**

The reason given for abandoning programmes of education and rehabilitation is overcrowding.

27. **A**

Answer D refers only to young offenders and the passage is not so limited. C's reference to rehabilitation programmes is inconsistent with the position taken in the passage. Sentence A has the same urgent tone adopted in the passage and is consistent with the passage's main theme. Recidivism means to go back to crime and levels of recidivism will not decline as long as our punishments fail to deter further offences.

28. **C**

The reason given for the lack of rehabilitation provision is overcrowding, but the criminal system's willingness or otherwise to provide resources for such provision is not discussed in the passage, nor can it be inferred.

Passage 8

29. **A**

Had the government been putting these contributions aside for the benefit of the pension holders then (assuming that the pensions are self-funding) there is no reason why the contributions should not be available to meet the commitments.

30. **D**

The passages states that 12 million are directly affected but also that the large numbers of people who contribute only a small amount to a private pension scheme are also at risk.

31. C
     The age of the migrants is not given and the pensioner–
     worker ratio would only be improved if the migrants were
     workers rather than pensioners.

32. B
     The passage concludes on the subject of workers with inade-
     quate private pension schemes, and therefore the follow-on
     sentence is most likely to be on that subject. Suggested answers B
     and D are the only sentences that continue that theme. But D can
     be rejected because no reference is made in the passage to long-
     awaited proposals on how to resolve the crisis.

Passage 9

33. A
     The estimates of spending against tax raised suggests a signif-
     icant deficit.

34. A
     That independence might involve significant challenges does not
     mean that it cannot be afforded. That price of independence
     might (or might not) be high but the Scottish people may be
     willing to afford it.

35. D
     Scotland, Ireland and Sweden are comparable in terms of popu-
     lation and geographic location in Europe, but the passage does
     not concern itself with this issue. It is reasonable to surmise that
     an independent Scotland would derive a greater percentage of its
     tax revenue from oil, and therefore that its economy would be
     more closely tied to that sector than currently.

36. C
     The passage only stated the level of tax revenue if Scotland were
     to be allocated the entire tax take from this sector. No infor-
     mation is provided on whether or not this is likely to occur
     should Scotland achieve independence.

Passage 10

37. A
     The passage states that youth unemployment is at a record level,
     so it can be taken to be at a level higher than in 1997.

38. E
    The passage states that opponents would place far greater emphasis on the family unit as one that comprises a married couple both of whom are living with their children, which would equally apply to gay couples caring for children and living in civil partnerships. Their concept of family would therefore include married couples or couples living in a civil partnership with children. None of the suggested answers includes both these groups.

39. C
    The date in which this allowance was abolished is not stated in the passage, nor can it be inferred from the passage.

40. D
    The opponent's are not against social cohesion but the ills that continue despite greater prosperity.

Further information

A great deal of information is available on the internet, and any search for terms such as UK government, UK Civil Service, Fast Stream will bring up many useful sites.

Job opportunities

All administrative grades
Jobcentre online: www.jobcentreplus.gov.uk/
Civil Service Recruitment Gateway: www.careers.civil-service.gov.uk/index

Information on the Fast Stream

www.faststream.gov.uk

The European Fast Stream
www.europeanfaststream.gov.uk

The GCHQ Fast Stream
www.gchq.gov.uk/recruitment /careers/

The Welsh Assembly Government Fast Stream
www.newydd.cymm.gov.uk/about/career_opportunities/
fast_stream/

The Scottish Parliament Fast Stream
www.careers-scotland.org.uk/
publicserviceadministrationfaststreamcivilservice

Information on the work of government

www.direct.gov.uk

Government Statistical Service
www.statistics.gov.uk

The Home Office
www.homeoffice.gov.uk

Free online practice tests can be found at:
www.shl.com
www.psl.com